5 DEVILS

That will kill Humanity

CA Harshil Mehta

BlueRose ONE
Stories Matter

First Published in July 2022

ISBN: 978-93-5611-420-3

BLUEROSE PUBLISHERS
www.BlueRoseONE.com
info@bluerosepublishers.com
+91 8882 898 898

Cover Design:
Geetika

Typographic Design:
Namrata Saini

Distributed by: BlueRose, Amazon, Flipkart

DEDICATION

This book is dedicated:

To my *Parents*- Striving hard to make you proud!

To my *late Nani*- For teaching me the Virtues of Goodness!

To *Humanity, Hope and Life*!

Shree Ganeshay Namah

5 Devils that will kill Humanity

In 1991, Michael Jackson, the King of Pop released a beautiful song titled 'Heal the world'. Following is a verse taken from the song:-

Heal the world
Make it a better place
For you and for me, and the entire human race
There are people dying
If you care enough for the living
Make a better place for you and for me

The song touched millions of hearts then and is still relevant till date as I see human values deteriorating with every passing day.

This world will surely be a good place if there are good people around us. Together, we can make this world a better place to live in provided we choose to keep something called humanity (insaniyat) alive within us.

CONTENTS

Introduction

St. Stephen high school is ranked among one of the best schools in Mumbai city. Every year, the students of this school excel in the field of academics, sports, performing arts, etc. Numerous awards have been won by the school; all credit goes to Mr. Mark David, the Principal of the school who is indeed a visionary leader, the knowledgeable teaching faculties, and all the brilliant students who put in extraordinary efforts to strive for perfection in whatever they do. Besides being one of the best, this school is also quite expensive and only students from affluent families could afford to study here. Most of the alumni of this school are extraordinarily successful in their respective professions.

12th January 2022, which is celebrated as National Youth Day in memory of Swami Vivekananda also marks the 50th anniversary of St. Stephen high school. Every year, on this occasion an annual program is organized by the school to celebrate the anniversary with much grandeur. Every year, besides having dancing, singing, and acting performances by the students, eminent personalities from different walks of life are invited as chief guests in the annual program. There is a small segment towards the end of the annual function wherein such esteemed guests, who have flourished in their respective fields, take the center stage and address the youth i.e. all the students of the school. The whole objective of this segment is to inspire and guide the youth on the right path so that today's youth can be prepared for tomorrow's world. In the past, renowned personalities like TV and film celebrities, musicians, famous sports people, and corporate leaders have attended the program and given motivational speeches, and shared their life experiences to help students get equipped with the right knowledge, skills, and wisdom to help them thrive in the real world that starts right outside the school gate.

For the upcoming annual program, the Principal has personally invited Mr. Anil Suri to be the chief guest and requested him to give a motivational speech to enlighten the students. Mr. Anil Suri is one of the most famous alumni of St. Stephen high school. He is a successful corporate leader, CEO of a very reputed FMCG company, and a generous philanthropist mainly known for his humanitarian work. More than his business achievements, he is highly respected for his social services and contribution to the social welfare of the society. Indeed, Mr. Anil Suri is known for his humility, kindness, and helpful nature.

On 20th December 2021, the Principal received an email confirmation from Mr. Anil Suri.

"Dear Mark David, Greetings! Hope you and your family members are in good health.

First of all, thank you so much for inviting me as a guest to the annual program. I am highly humbled and honored. It's been really long since I visited my school. I will definitely attend the annual program on 12th January 2022 at 6 pm. This would be a great opportunity for me to interact with today's youth. You expect me to inspire your students and guide them in the right direction, but I don't know how qualified I am to do that. Nevertheless, I still would like to give a small speech on the topic '5 Devils' Hope that serves the purpose.

Once again, thanks for the invitation. Looking forward to a great event.

Take care!

Regards,

Anil Suri"

After reading the email, the Principal was absolutely delighted; he knows how busy Mr. Suri is owing to his work commitments. Mr. David got excited as well as a little curious thinking about the topic name '5 Devils'. However, he didn't overanalyze. The next morning, in the school auditorium, he announced that Mr. Anil Suri is going to be the guest for the upcoming annual program. This elated everyone present there. Though Anil Suri is not some Bollywood celebrity or a sports personality, yet he is a renowned public figure in the society and highly revered for his work ethic, integrity, and social welfare services.

As the days passed by, the preparation was going on in full swing. Students were super excited and doing their rehearsals of singing and dancing daily, teachers and other supporting staff were busy coordinating with event managers to make all the necessary arrangements for the event. They were leaving no stone unturned to make it a grand and enjoyable event.

THE CELEBRATION DAY

Finally, the day arrived, 12th January 2022, the 50th anniversary of St. Stephen high school, one of the best schools in Mumbai. The entire school was beautifully decorated with colorful balloons, flowers, ribbons, and sparkling lights. All the participating students had arrived much before the event time and were busy with their rehearsals. The event was supposed to start at 6 pm. All the parents started arriving from 5 pm onwards and got themselves seated in the beautifully decorated auditorium. They were super excited to see their lovely kids perform on stage like rockstars.

At around 5:45 pm, suddenly there was some commotion observed near the entrance gate as a few teachers and other volunteers gathered there. A black Mercedes car halted at the entrance and Mr. Anil Suri steps out of the car. He looked absolutely sharp and dashing in a black suit just like those models who appear in clothing brand advertisements on television. He looked physically fit and much younger than his age which was more than fifty-five. The teachers and all the volunteers, not that they went crazy on seeing him, like how normal people behave after seeing a Bollywood celebrity but out of immense respect, they welcomed their guest with complete dignity and grace. Mr. Suri with a gentle smile on his face greeted everyone cordially and took his seat in the front row of the auditorium.

As St. Stephen is known for its discipline, the program commenced sharp at 6 pm with Mr. Mark David taking the center stage and welcoming all the attendees including the guest of honor, Mr. Anil Suri. A small video clip was shown to the audience highlighting the achievements of Mr. Suri, and then the event started with a bang.

Numerous dances, singing, and acting performances were given by all the students right from 1st grade to 10th grade. Most of the students grooved to Bollywood songs. Even a talent round was organized where students showcased their different talents like mimicry, playing musical instruments, reciting poems, etc.

The crowd was ecstatic, enjoying every performance, Mr. Suri was having a good time too. The air was filled with a high level of euphoria, kids had set the stage on fire with their energetic dance moves. The show went on for around 3 hrs. The last performance of the event got over around 9 pm.

And then comes the most awaited segment, a session by the Guest of Honor Mr. Suri. '5 Devils', the topic itself was very intriguing. The Principal invited Mr. Suri onto the stage, highlighted all his professional accomplishments, and handed over the mike to him. The entire audience seemed more excited than before. The opening lines by Mr. Suri were as follows:-

"Dear Mark David sir, all the teachers, supremely talented kids, and their proud parents, good evening everyone. My heart is filled with immense joy to have witnessed a great show like this. Thanks a lot for the invitation, principal sir; I thoroughly enjoyed each and every performance. Heartiest congratulations to all these wonderful kids for putting up such a great show. This has taken me back to my school days, I am feeling really nostalgic. The enormous amount of talent, passion, and enthusiasm that I just saw on the stage has amazed me beyond words. Honestly speaking, I was not even five percent of it when I was in school. Sitting there, I was wondering how would I motivate all these self-motivated students who are already a powerhouse of energy and positivity? I am not a very great motivational speaker but still today I will make a sincere attempt to share something valuable with you all, especially with the youth. I hope I don't bore you guys. I am almost sixty years old and I'm not sure how successful I am, I feel that there's still a long way to go. But I'm certainly very happy and love my life, this is because I followed the advice of my mother. That advice worked wonders for me and it filled my life with an abundance of joy. I'm sure that this advice if lived by, would bring similar results to you all."

(Everyone present in the auditorium was listening to Mr. Suri very attentively)

"So, today I am going to talk about 5 devils. I was introduced to these devils by my mother when I was in school and now it's time for me to introduce all you school kids to these 5 devils. So are you all ready?"

"Yeahhh!!!"...the students and their parents cheered in excitement

Since childhood, my mother always told me that 'har insaan mein acchai bhi hoti hai aur burai bhi'. Both angels and devils reside in each of us. Both are bitter enemies and constantly fight to overpower each other. One day, very innocently I asked "Mom, if both fight with each other, who wins. Who is more powerful, the angel or the devil?" To which my mom replied, "Son, it depends on who you support. Whoever you feed more, will become more powerful and eventually win" "Then whom should I support", I asked my mom. "Son, Devils are more attractive, compelling, and manipulative, they will try harder compared to angels to control your mind. There are high chances that your mind will get influenced faster by devils than angels and you may end up supporting devils. But if you allow devils to win, you will lose everything like money, relationships, health, and respect. And somehow if you manage to avoid the devil's trap and support angels and help them win, you will win everything in life including money, relationships, health, and respect. "Ok mom, I have clearly understood that no matter what, I don't have to support devils. But please tell me who these devils are? "These devils are very dangerous, you may think of them as very small and harmless but they are so dangerous that if they keep winning over angels in every individual, humanity will be killed. Anil, let me introduce you to 5 devils that reside within us and if we allow them to win, one day they will kill humanity" my mom said.

By now, the entire audience in the auditorium was completely engrossed in Anil's speech. Mr. Anil is a powerful orator and has exemplary public speaking skills. He knows how to charm people with his words and persona. This has been one of the major reasons for his success in his personal, social, and professional life. Mr. Anil continued with his session.

"Friends, I hope you guys are not getting bored"

"Noooooo" the audience cheered.

So, without wasting any further time, let me introduce you all to the first Devil.

DEVIL ONE

Anger

In Bhagavad Gita, it's written that 'Anger leads to clouding of judgment, which results in bewilderment of the memory. When the memory is bewildered, the intellect gets destroyed; and when the intellect is destroyed, one is ruined' Let me simplify this, anger will always impair your judgment, because of which people commit certain mistakes and regret them later. When your judgment is impaired, it will adversely affect your memory and state of mind leading to loss of intellect. When you lose your intellect, you will lose your inner conscience and forget the difference between right and wrong. Most often you will end up doing wrong things. Accumulation of all these wrong things will eventually destroy your life. Anger will impair your ability to differentiate bad from the good. Devils are always more proactive than angels, so the devil of anger will force your mind to do the wrong thing giving you a temporary sense of satisfaction, but you will not realize at that moment that this temporary sense of satisfaction will lead to a permanent disaster in your life. We all are humans and we will get into situations in our life that will make us angry. Sometimes getting angry is beyond our control as this is basic human nature. It is absolutely normal but how we react in that fit of rage will determine our future. I have seen many relationships getting destroyed because of anger, best of best friends turning into worst enemies because of anger, businesses getting collapsed because of bad decisions taken in anger, the health of individuals getting ruined because of anger. I have seen humans losing their humanity because of anger.

I was in 2nd grade when I was first introduced to these devils by my mother. She used to remind me about these devils once every month to make sure that I never forget them. She also explained why it is so important for me to destroy them before they destroy my happiness.

I think the best way to convey a message is through a story, so would you all like to hear a story?

"Yes," the audience instantly replied.

So, friends, let me share a very interesting story that I had read somewhere with all of you.

"There was a little boy named Rohit who had a very bad temper. He used to get angry really fast over petty things and react in an inconsiderate manner. One day his father got a bag of nails and a hammer and asked Rohit to hammer one nail on the fence every time he lost his temper and minced harsh words.

On the first day, Rohit hammered thirty nails. As days passed by, the number of nails on the fence started reducing as Rohit was learning to control his anger. One day, Rohit didn't lose his temper at all and no nails were hammered on the fence. He immediately went to his father and shared this achievement with him. His father was delighted and now suggested Rohit to remove one nail from the fence every time he was able to suppress his anger. Every day Rohit used to remove a few nails from the fence as by now he had learned the art of anger management. After a few weeks, finally, he was able to remove all the nails from the fence. He was super excited and again shared this new achievement with his father. His father was very pleased and congratulated him for winning the battle against this Devil anger. The father then asked Rohit to observe the holes that were created on the fence due to hammering. He said," Son, I am proud of you for conquering your anger. But these holes on the fence will remain forever and the fence will never look like before. Similarly in life, whenever you say harsh words to people in anger, you may hurt them to such an extent that the scars of your words might remain forever and your relationship with that person would never be the same"

As soon as the story got over, the audience loved it so much that all of them started applauding. More than the story, it was the impactful and thought-provoking manner in which Mr. Suri narrated that mesmerized everyone. Mr. Suri continued...

So friends, remember that tongue wounds more than a lance. Words spoken in anger to someone can sometimes cause irreparable damage. Hence, think twice before you speak. Don't let the devil within you overshadow your goodness. Don't let the devil within you kill humanity. Besides being injurious to your relationships, anger is also injurious to your health. So let me teach you some ways through which you can fight this devil. What can be done in the moment of anger to minimize its damage:

- As they say, silence is golden, whenever you are angry, practice silence for a while. Don't react instantly because a mindless reaction may put you in more trouble.
- Do a bit of exercise to relax your mind. Go for a walk or do some body stretching, this will calm you down.
- Start doing something that gives you joy like listening to music, reading, watching a movie, etc.
- Practice gratitude. Focus on what's right when you feel that everything is wrong. Thinking about the good things you've been blessed with will help you neutralize the anger.
- Practice empathy, try to walk in the other person's shoes, and see the situation from their perspective.
- Start looking out for solutions for your problems. Every time you find a solution, a portion of your anger will get doused.

It's absolutely normal to get angry, this is basic human emotion, but don't let the devil within you influence your actions and words.

So, friends, I hope you had a good time meeting the first devil. (*Audience started laughing*).

Now it's time for me to introduce the second devil. He's been waiting in the queue for so long.

DEVIL TWO

The name of the second devil that resides within us is ***'Arrogance'***

Arrogance

Let me start with a story from Mahabharata. When the battle of Kurukshetra was at its peak, Arjuna and Karna were constantly fighting and shooting arrows at each other. When Arjuna would shoot his arrow, Karna's chariot would go back by 20-25 feet. And when Karna would shoot his arrow, Arjuna's chariot would shake a bit and go back by 3-5 feet. Lord Krishna would applaud Karna every time his arrow hit Arjuna's chariot but never applauded Arjuna when his arrow hit. At the end of the day, Arjuna asked Lord Krishna," Oh Lord, I shot so many arrows at Karna's chariot but not once did you appreciate me. Lord Krishna replied," Oh Arjuna, your chariot is protected by Hanuman who is sitting on top of your chariot's flag, Sheshnag who is at the wheel, and me as your charioteer leading from the front. But Karna's chariot was not protected by any such divine force yet he fought so bravely. After the battle was over, Lord Krishna got off the chariot after Arjuna stepped down and as soon as Lord Krishna stepped down, the chariot caught fire and turned into dust. Lord Krishna said to Arjuna. "Oh Arjuna, see your chariot was destroyed by Karna a long time ago, it was the divine force that was protecting it from getting destroyed"

So friends what do we learn from the story? All your achievements in life, besides hard work, are a result of Divine intervention, and the moment you start becoming arrogant about it, very soon your achievements will turn into dust. I've seen many people destroying their lives in arrogance. It's hard to be successful in real life but it's even harder to not let that success go to your head. A few days back, I met Rahul in my building's elevator. Rahul stays in my building and is a young schoolboy studying in 8th grade. He looked extremely delighted and when I asked him the reason for his happiness, he said," Anil uncle, I scored 94% in my school exam and once again I am the topper of my class" I said," Congratulations beta, so good to hear that. What has made you happier, scoring 94% or becoming a topper?" "Becoming the topper of my class gives me more happiness" Rahul replied. "And why is that", I politely asked. Rahul said," Anil uncle, for the last 3 years I've been the topper of my class consistently scoring more marks than others. It feels amazing to be the best. After all, scoring more marks will help me be more successful in life than others!" After this statement, Rahul's floor came, he stepped outside the elevator and went.

I have spoken to Rahul's parents many times hence I know how hard-working and studious he is. I have even spoken to Rahul many times in the past but this time he sounded slightly arrogant and overconfident in his tone. That day I heard not Rahul but the devil within him speaking.

I have observed that in school, success is generally measured by your marks, students scoring more marks are appreciated and respected more by teachers. I'm sure most of the students over here would be having this false belief that scoring more marks will guarantee prosperity in life. Tell me honestly, how many students over here think this way? *(more than 50% of students raised their hands)* As expected, and now how many parents and teachers over here think this way? (most of the parents started laughing) Well, I get my answer in your laughter. (Parents and teachers started laughing even more) Friends, your marks play a very negligible role in determining your success in real life. If marks can't guarantee that then why arrogance. Some people are too arrogant about their looks. I can see some really beautiful people sitting in the audience. I want to share one important secret with all the beautiful people seated here but it's my humble request to keep this a secret and not let this go out of this auditorium. Sooner or later unless you are Anil Kapoor or an incarnation of Anil Kapoor, your good looks will eventually fade like a flower. (The audience erupted in laughter once again) How many of you knew this before? (Everyone including small kids showed their affirmation) Wow, I'm a little disappointed, I thought that I am going to share some new never heard before facts with all of you. So, everyone including these little kids knows that your looks are not permanent and will eventually fade away then why arrogance. And the biggest catalyst of all to awaken the devil of arrogance within you is MONEY. Wealthy people are arrogant about their wealth for they think that wealth makes them more powerful than others. Arrogance lead to a false belief of superiority over others and because of this people become overconfident about their material possessions. Time and again I've seen people's wealth perishing when they start becoming arrogant. I have seen many *roadpatis* becoming *crorepatis* and *crorepatis* overnight becoming *roadpatis*. A little success in your professional life can awaken the devil within you. Beware of this devil, it can destroy you. Wealth goes faster than it comes. If the wealth you earn is not permanent then why arrogance.

Your money is not permanent,

Your friends are not permanent, and it takes no time for friends to become enemies.

Your looks are not permanent.

Your good health is not permanent.

Your life is not permanent.

When your life itself is not permanent then why arrogance.

Friends, there is a very thin line between confidence and arrogance, never cross it. Never allow the devil of arrogance to overpower you.

Complete silence prevailed in the auditorium for 10-15 seconds. By now the crowd was completed engrossed in the session. It looked as if all the parents and teachers in the audience began introspecting and recalled the times when they might have done something regretful under the influence of this devil.

Mr. Anil continued…

Sometimes in life, because of arrogance, despite earning a lot of wealth, people get poorer and poorer when they start losing priceless treasures like true friendship, trust, respect, relationships, and goodwill. By the time they realize, the damage becomes irreparable, losses become irrecoverable and the pain of regret becomes incurable.

(Audience started applauding with an emotional and heartfelt smile on their faces)

So, friends, I hope you had a good meeting with this devil too. It's time to introduce the third devil. This devil is closely related to the second devil almost like a brother.

DEVIL THREE

His name is ***EGO***

Ego is humanity's biggest enemy. Having an inflated ego can destroy your relationships, it can destroy your career, and it can destroy your life. Let us understand the meaning of the word ego. How many of you are Salman Khan fans?

(A majority of the crowd raised their hands in excitement) and how many of you have seen his movie 'Ready' *(Everyone raised their hands including people who hadn't raised their hands for the previous question.)*

It has a dialogue in which Salman says, '*Zindagi mein 3 cheezon ko kabhi underestimate mat karna,* ***"I"***, ***"Me"*** *and*

"Myself" (The crowd burst out laughing). In simple words, ego is nothing but an obsession with 'I, Me, and Myself'. Let me narrate a short story.

Once upon a time, there was a man named Vishwa who was a painter. He lived in a small town and made his living selling paintings daily. Every morning he used to go out along with his paintings in search of customers and return by evening after selling them. All his life he continued with the same occupation. In the earlier years, his paintings were merely sold for Rs100-200 per unit but in the later stage of his life, his paintings fetched around Rs800. As he grew old, his vision started fading and he became weak. He decided to take retirement and teach painting to his son Arjun so that he can continue the business. Like his father, even Arjun followed the same routine of going out early morning with the paintings, selling them to customers, and returning in the evening. But in the initial days, Arjun was not able to sell the paintings for more than Rs100 per unit. He expressed his concern to his father. His father taught him some new methods through which he could make his paintings better. Arjun implemented those methods and now he was able to fetch Rs300 per painting.

Still, he was not satisfied as his father used to get Rs800. Again, his father taught him some new techniques to improve the design and color pattern of the painting. With this, now Arjun started earning Rs600 per painting but still, he was unhappy as he couldn't reach the 800 mark. His father once again taught him better techniques and ensured that he puts in extra effort every day to practice them. One day, Arjun came home super excited and told his father that he sold a painting for Rs1000. Arjun's happiness knew no bounds. His father was also equally happy.

As days passed by, there was a slight change in Arjun's attitude. He stopped seeking advice from his father. One day his father said, "Arjun I am very proud of you that you are now able to sell a painting for Rs1000. Let me teach you some more useful techniques that will help you to sell paintings for Rs1500" to which Arjun replied," Father, in your entire life, you have not earned a single rupee more than Rs800 per painting. I have already surpassed the 800 mark. I don't think your techniques will be of any further help" Listening to this, his father said" Son, my father passed away 15 years ago, and since then I wasn't able to sell a painting for more than Rs800. The maximum amount that my father was able to earn in his life per painting was Rs500. When I surpassed his score, I stopped paying attention to his advice as I started considering myself superior to him. Ever since then, my ego didn't allow me to progress any further. I guarantee that if you don't change your attitude, even 20 years from now you will still be earning only Rs1000 per painting. When a person starts feeding his ego, he stops growing and starts losing because he thinks too highly of himself and underestimates others"

Ego means giving too much importance to yourself and behaving as if you are superior to others. Your attitude of superiority will make you start expecting from others. When you expect a lot and others don't live up to it, it hurts your ego to such an extent that you develop a feeling of hatred towards others. And hatred is enough to kill all humanity and compassion within you. Let me give some examples:-

- Why should I say sorry?

- Why should I call my friend, can't he call me?
- Why should I seek help from my colleagues?
- Why should I seek help from a female? *(Male ego)*
- Why should I listen to my junior?
- Why should I say thank you? He never does.
- Why should I congratulate someone? He never does.
- Why should I wish him on birthdays? He never does.
- Why should I help him? He never did.

Let me ask a question to all the parents and teachers seated here, please do answer it truthfully. How many of you have lost touch with your school and college friends mainly because of ego, thinking "Why should I call him, can't he call me?

Think for a while, ask yourself and answer truthfully.

(Almost 50% of hands went up)

The gentleman in red shirt seated in 3rd row, do you mind sharing your experience with us.

Gentleman: Hello Mr. Anil, I am Rakesh. Yes, I have lost touch with my friend who used to be my best friend in school.

"And the reason was?" asked Anil.

Rakesh: Actually after school, both of us took admission in different colleges. He got busy with his new friends and new life and gradually we lost touch. He never really bothered to contact me despite having a beautiful friendship in school. Maybe it was because of his ego. He wanted to show that he had found better friends and is busy with them.

Anil: Sir, how many times did you put effort to contact him after school?

Rakesh: Well, I tried a few times but he didn't seem interested. Moreover, I could sense those egoistic vibes. Hence, even I stopped contacting him.

Anil: Thank you Mr. Rakesh for sharing your experience, you may please sit down.

Misunderstanding and wrong assumptions can destroy any relationship. Mr. Rakesh assumed that because his friend is not taking the initiative, he wouldn't be interested in keeping a friendship. Similarly, his friend might have assumed that because Rakesh is not putting enough efforts, he would've gotten busy with his new friends and new life. There were no calls, no messages. One was in ego, the other one was in hope. To sustain any form of relationship, it is important to practice selflessness. The moment you start expecting from others, the relationship will lose its sanctity. Humility is the oxygen that keeps a relationship alive. Only humility can kill the ego. Be humble, no matter what the circumstances are. One day humility shall win over ego. It requires courage and a big heart to take initiative. Drop all the egos, because no one is superior to anyone. Remember, there is only one force that was, is, and will always be superior to all of us and that is the almighty.

Stop expecting from others and start expecting from yourself, be a leader, be humble, be considerate, starve your ego, feed humility, respect others and kill the other person's ego with your kindness.

(Once again, the audience started giving thunderous applause and were in absolute awe of Mr.Anil's charisma)

Friends, even I have seen failures. I have gone through several rough patches of life and it was all because of ego. Even the tiniest seed of ego can hamper your growth in life. Don't let the seed of ego grow within you. I was fortunate that at a very early stage of life, I uprooted it from my system and it has helped me become a better human being.

All the wonderful kids here, don't you all want to be good human beings when you grow up?

"Yes", the kids cheered.

Then all you need to do is drop your.....*(kids shouted EGOOOO)*. That's right, you must drop your ego to fly high.

It's time to say goodbye to ego and welcome a new devil.

DEVIL FOUR

Let's welcome devil no. 4: **Greed**

Mahatma Gandhi, the father of our nation, once said," The world has enough for everyone's need, but not enough for everyone's greed."

In Bhagavad Gita, Lord Krishna says, "There are three gates leading to the hell of self-destruction for the soul- lust, anger, and greed. Therefore, all should abandon these three.

Let me narrate a short story.

Rohan, Shyam, and Mohit were best friends. They lived in a city and had been friends since childhood. One day they decide to go for a picnic. Early morning, they went to the nearby mountain for trekking. On reaching the top, they set their tents and got comfortable. Throughout the day, they enjoyed the beauty of nature. In the evening, while they were returning, they found a bag full of gold lying in the middle of the road. Seeing that, all three of them got super excited. They decide to share the gold equally among them. On their way home, they felt hungry so Mohit asked Rohan to go to a nearby shop to get some food. While Rohan was away arranging food for his friends, Mohit and Shyam conspired to kill Rohan so that they could get more share of the gold. Both of them became victims of the devil Greed.

But, even Rohan was not spared by the devil, he poisoned the food packets to kill both his friends so that he could enjoy the entire gold. When Rohan arrived, he was brutally attacked by his friends and he lay dead. Both Shyam and Mohit were super delighted thinking that each of them would get a larger share of the gold. They started gobbling the food that Rohan had brought for them. After some time, the poison kicked in and even they died, leaving all the gold on the ground unclaimed.

Just like how greed killed Rohan, Shyam, and Mohit, similarly in today's world greed is killing humanity. Greed for excess wealth, greed for extra power, greed for fame, etc destroy everything. Greed is born when one starts comparing their life with others. Greed is born when gratitude dies.

Often, I meet unhappy souls who are too busy finding flaws in others or complaining about their life that they forget to appreciate all the great things they've been blessed with. Be grateful, for you have been blessed with good health, be grateful, for you can walk, talk, see, touch, feel, be grateful, for you have been blessed with wonderful parents, be grateful, for you have been blessed with caring friends, be grateful, for you have been blessed with a shelter to live under, be grateful, for you all are alive today. These days people are too busy pursuing their greed that they fail to acknowledge all the beautiful blessings they have in life.

The only weapon that can kill the devil Greed is Gratitude. Gratitude is the antidote for Greed.

Friends, leave no opportunity to practice gratitude. Many people think that practicing gratitude and being content with what you have often hampers your progress. A little greed is healthy as long as it fuels your ambition and helps you prosper in life. Let me explain the difference between Greed and Ambition.

The dictionary meaning of the word Greed is," a selfish or excessive desire for more than is needed or deserved" whereas the word ambition means "desire and determination to achieve success"

Friends, there are two types of success: - Inner success and Outer success. If you chase inner success, that is called ambition but the moment you start chasing outer success, your ambition will turn into greed.

Outer success is about doing or achieving things to make people around you think that you are successful. It is more like trying to meet the perception of success set by the outside world. It is an endeavor to accomplish things so that people in your neighborhood can be convinced about your success. Greed makes you chase success, not for your own satisfaction but to impress people around you. In pursuit of outer success, people are often blinded by greed and lose humanity on their way. And, once you lose basic human values, your destruction is certain.

On a contrary, **Inner success** is about doing things and chasing goals that give you immense satisfaction and a sense of fulfillment regardless of what the world thinks about it. It can be anything like learning new skills, cultivating the right habits, expanding your knowledge, utilizing time productively, or making small but consistent progress daily. Inner success is succeeding for personal growth and development and not to please the outside world.

I always advise people to chase inner success because ultimately personal happiness is all that matters. In outer success, you compare your life with others, and comparison gives birth to greed. Greed will never allow you to be at peace because there is no end to it.

So, friends, four devils have been introduced so far, how many of you had fun meeting these devils?

(Almost everyone in the audience raised their hands),

wow… it feels good to see that you guys had too much fun meeting the devils, how many of you already knew about these devils?

(Most of the parents and teachers raised their hands however young kids were slightly unsure and hence did not react)

Great! It means I have not shared anything new. The majority of you already knew, now the most important question, 'How many of you have become victims of these 4 devils in the past?'

(Only a few hands amongst the adult population go up)

Oh. Very few, this is an indication that many times in life, we do certain things despite knowing that it's not going to do any good to anyone.

As they say, save the best for the last, it's time for the last devil to enter the scene. This devil is the strongest of all. It is nearly impossible to evade this devil. I'm sure that every individual in this auditorium, has, at some point in time, been a victim of this devil.

DEVIL FIVE

Here I present the 5th and the biggest devil of all '**Jealousy**'

My dear friends, Jealousy is a terrible disease, even deadlier than cancer. A quick question for all these wonderful school kids and better be honest, how many of you feel jealous of your classmates when they score more marks than you?

(Primary students were too innocent to react to this question hence they didn't raise their hands. Secondary students being slightly more mature started thinking and looking at their friends. Probably all of them knew the answer but were not sure if it was a wise thing to raise their hands. However, after a few seconds, few students mustered the courage

to raise their hands. Their courage inspired many more to express the truth. More hands went up)

See I told you all, no one is spared by this devil. I'm sure that the younger kids will soon become victims of it too.

Let me narrate a short story, I hope all of you, especially the kids like listening to stories.

"Yes!!", the audience cheered

Rohan and Shiv were best friends, studying in the same class. They've been together since junior kg. Shiv always used to be ahead of Rohan in terms of studies, sports, and other extra-curricular activities. Rohan always tried outperforming Shiv but never succeeded. In front of Shiv, Rohan always behaved very normally and friendly but behind his back, he resented Shiv's success. Slowly, the devil started appearing in between their friendship. One day, Rohan was very sad and the cause of his sadness was extreme jealousy. He had a gloomy face and tears were rolling down his cheeks. On seeing her son in tears, his mother immediately came to his rescue and enquired about the problem to which Rohan said, 'Mom, it's all because of Shiv. Once again, he scored more marks than me and got all the appreciation from teachers and other classmates. Why can't I beat him?' 'Do you feel jealous of him' the mother asked. 'No, he is my friend, I am not jealous but it really hurts when others who are just like you get better results. Even I want better results!' Rohan replied. 'Son, just remember the rule of life, ***it gives you not what you want but what you deserve***. If Shiv scores better marks than you, it means he would be doing something better than you. The last time when I had a word with Shiv's mom, she said that he prepares a day-wise timetable and follows it diligently. He divides his time effectively between studies and play. During exam days, he gives first priority to studies and eliminates TV, social media, and other digital distractions from his life. And most important of all, he studies daily. Daily revision of what is being taught in school makes his life much easier during exam days unlike you who pick up books only when the exam is around the corner. If he is your best friend, why don't you admire all the good qualities in him and appreciate it? Have you ever tried ascertaining the reason behind his good performance?' the mother asked.

That's when Rohan realizes that he always used to envy Shiv's good performance but never really tried finding the reason behind his success. He always had the desire to score better marks than Shiv but never really replicated Shiv's discipline in his life. Most of his time and energy were wasted envying others' success. One day he decides that instead of wasting his time and energy envying Shiv's progress, he would inculcate discipline in his life. He will rid himself of all bad habits and cultivate productive habits just like Shiv. He started planning his days in advance and divided his time between study and recreation. He made sure that he never skipped his daily revision. During the exam days, he never allowed his mind to wander anywhere else and focused only on his studies.

One day when Rohan returned home after school, his face was beaming with happiness. When asked by his mother, he replied "Mom, I am super delighted today as I got the results of my exam. I have come second in the class"

'Who came first?', his mother asked. "Shiv", Rohan replied. "Aren't you jealous of him as once again he scored better marks than you?", the mother asks. "No Mom, I am too busy rejoicing thinking about my progress that, I don't have time to envy others. And anyways Mom, I have realized that earlier I didn't perform well because most of the time I wasted my precious time and energy, envying Shiv. But this time, I used the same time and energy for my personal development. I studied harder than before and hence God rewarded me with better results. I will always live life by this rule ***"Life gives you not what you want but what you deserve"*** If somebody is more successful than me, it means he is more deserving. Definitely, he would've done something different and more than me. Instead of feeling jealous, I will learn from him and make myself worthy of good results. At least, it will help me outperform myself, if not others."

Listening to this, Rohan's mother had a big smile on her face, for now, she knew that her son has killed the biggest devil called Jealousy.

It is very natural to feel envious of others' progress, that's human nature but friends, envy will never serve your progress. In fact, the more you envy others, the lesser will be your progress. When I started my career as a corporate employee, for the first couple of years, my colleagues got better increments and they got promoted faster than me. Of course, it hurts when you see people who started their journey just like you as a fresher climbing the success ladder faster. But then, my mom's words of wisdom came to my rescue, she always said," ***Son, you have got two choices, either you become a slave of your internal devils and***

live your life like a lifeless person, or win over those devils and live like a King" I made a choice to not live my life like a slave but like a king. And since then, I have always tried to admire the good qualities in others and learned immensely from them. Life certainly is biased because it discriminates between the worthy and unworthy. Jealousy will always keep you unworthy but admiring the right people and learning from them will set you up on the path toward worthiness.

More men die of jealousy than of cancer- Joseph P Kennedy

So, friends, these are the 5 devils within humans, which are very much capable of killing humanity- **Anger, Arrogance, Ego, Greed, and Jealousy.** My mother passed on this information to me at a very young age and always reminded me of them at regular intervals so that I don't forget. I try to pass on this to as many people as possible. Whenever people out of all curiosity ask me to share some secrets of success, my answer remains as simple as ABC, 'kill these 5 devils - **Anger, Arrogance, Ego, Greed, and jealousy,** and see yourself onward and upward onto the path of eternal prosperity'

Q AND A

With this, the most awaited session '5 devils that will kill humanity' of Mr. Anil Suri came to an end followed by a thunderous round of applause. The entire auditorium was charged up with positivity and the joyous expressions on the audience's faces were a testimony to Mr. Anil's ability to mesmerize the crowd. Simple things were explained in an extravagant fashion. Most often, people want to know how to become successful but Mr. Anil enlightened everyone on how not to fail in life. Devils could derail us from the path of success. The entire session lasted for about 45 minutes and the audience did not feel bored even for a single minute.

Mark David, the principal boards the stage to express his gratitude towards Mr. Anil Suri.

"I want to take this opportunity to thank Mr. Anil Suri on behalf of everyone present here. Despite being a busy man, it's very kind and generous of him to spare some time out of his busy schedule to attend this event. Mr. Anil, when it was announced to our students that this year's annual program is going to be graced by your presence, literally their happiness knew no bounds. They started counting days for they were super excited to meet you. In the past, we've had some Bollywood and sports personalities attend our event, but never did I see such a euphoria. Bollywood stars have become famous by acting and dancing, and sports personalities have become famous by playing and winning but you, Mr. Anil, have become famous by serving humanity. People like you are rare, and the world needs more like you. Surely with your presence," *Yahaa iss mehfil mein chaar chand lag gaye hai*" I'm sure the students over here have immensely learned from your words of wisdom and will surely kill the 5 devils you spoke about. Some of them don't want to let this opportunity of interacting with you go to waste. They have a few questions and they would be super delighted if you could answer them personally. With your permission, can we have a small QandA segment?"

Mr. Anil with a very affectionate smile replies:

"Sir, *nekii aur pooch pooch.* First of all, thank you very much for your kind and respectful words. I truly believe ***that real success is not in having a high bank balance but in reserving a small place in people's hearts***. Respect is something that can't be bought, it can only be earned. Real fame is not when people remember you for your wealth and power but for your goodness. Whenever I attend such events, I always endeavor to learn more from the youth of this generation than they can from me. I leave no opportunity to interact with young minds as their minds are always full of curiosity and curiosity creates history. Looking forward to all their questions and will be happy to answer them"

Miss Divya, the history teacher, came forward and volunteered to be the moderator for the QandA segment. She opened up the session and many hands went up in a fraction of a second. Surely too many questions were bottled up within the curious minds of these kids.

Kids of lower grades were given first priority to express themselves and the mike was handed over to a little boy seated in the third row.

Innocent Aditya

Q. Hi Anil sir, my name is Aditya and I study in 4th grade. I am a big fan of yours (*He said in a very cute and adorable manner with the innocence of childhood*) My mother scolds me when I get less marks. You are sooo successful, have you ever scored less marks in school?

The audience burst out laughing

Anil: Hi Aditya, you are very cute. Not only have I scored less marks but also have failed twice in chemistry subject. I never liked chemistry. But one day I realized that my poor performance is due to my careless attitude. My mother told me that Anil, scoring less marks is ok but a careless attitude is not at all acceptable. Don't study for marks but for knowledge, change your attitude not for better marks but for a better life because real life starts outside the school gate. Then instead of focusing on marks, I started focusing on the knowledge. Learning became fun and gradually my marks improved. Often, I pass on my mother's advice to school kids. Study for the knowledge that will help you in your life that starts outside the school gate. And for this, it is important to have the right attitude. So, Aditya, you don't like studying?

Aditya: I like sports more than studies but my mother does not encourage me in sports.

Anil: This is one of the big reasons why kids don't like studying because they are forced to study for scoring more marks instead of gaining knowledge. And if kids show interest in fields other than studies such as sports, dance, etc. they are discouraged. They are always told to prioritize studies over everything else. I believe that you must first prioritize what you love rather than what others want. I know many people who were not good at studies because their passion resided somewhere else. Some of them got support from their parents and have prospered while others didn't and are still struggling. Real prosperity is not measured by the amount of money in your bank account but by the amount of happiness and satisfaction in your mind. Some of my friends regret not doing what they wanted and the only advice I give them is to allow their kids to do what they want. I request all the parents seated here, especially Aditya's mother to please allow your kids to pursue their interests. You should be concerned if your kids have no interests at all. Failure in school exams doesn't mean failure in life, but failure to follow your heart may lead to failure in life. Aditya, you can smile now because I'm sure your mother will now encourage you in sports. But promise me that when the exams come, you will focus more on your studies than anything else. Also, study for knowledge and not for marks.

Aditya: Thank you so much Anil sir, I promise I will study more during exams and play more in vacation. (*And saying this, Aditya sat down with a smile on his face*)

Key takeaways

A simple answer to a simple question. Two effective messages are conveyed through a simple answer. First, things should be learned bearing in mind not the end result but daily personal growth. As they say, success is not a destination but a journey to enjoy. If progress can make you feel happy, then every day is an opportunity to rejoice since progress can be made daily no matter how big or small it is. Knowledge that can help us live a better life is far better than the knowledge required to score marks. Also, learning is not restricted only to school and college but is a lifelong process. A day without learning is a day wasted.

The second message is all about doing things you like so that life can be lived without regrets. The sand of time waits for no one. Making correct use of your time produces results, whereas time wasted produces regrets. A person who lives with regrets dies daily. Therefore, it is very important to discover your passion, earlier the better, so that you can set life goals in alignment with your passion and channel all your energies in the right direction. Work doesn't feel like work when you work on something that you enjoy the most. Parents can play an instrumental role in helping their kids discover their passion. Kids may have flair for different things like dance, sports, singing, public speaking, writing, studies, etc., but it is the responsibility of the parents and teachers to nurture the passion of their kids. Just like how daily watering, sunlight, and a positive environment contribute to the growth and development of the plant, similarly, our passion requires daily nourishment. A person's self-esteem will be at its peak when he decides to tread the path of his choice. No amount of failure can shake your self-belief if you are totally convinced of your passion. Parents and teachers should not choose a career path for kids but rather act as mentors and guide them once they choose a path for themselves.

Degree is just a piece of paper; real education is seen in your behavior.

Devils: Required or Not

Q. Hi Anil sir, my name is Alwin D'Souza, and I study in 6th grade. I truly enjoyed your session about 5 devils. Even I believe that anger, ego, and arrogance can lead to self-destruction but don't you think a little bit of jealousy and greed is required in today's competitive world to succeed. Our teachers always say that if you are not competitive, you are lazy and laziness leads to no progress.

Anil: Hi Alwin, that's a nice line: laziness leads to no progress. I distinctly remember that when I was a student of this school, my English teacher Miss Sarah Fernandes, the teacher whom I admired the most, often said that "Kids, in life, if you lose wealth, you have lost nothing, if you lose health, you have lost something but if you ever lose your character, you would lose everything. "Alwin, it's very good to be competitive but I don't think jealousy and greed are required for that competitive spirit. When you envy someone, let's say your friend who has scored more marks than you, you waste your time and energy thinking about your friend's progress, the more you think about it, the more distracted you will be in your life. Your feeling of jealousy is in no way going to affect your friend's performance because he will get what he deserves, but jealousy will surely deteriorate your focus and performance in life. When you start feeling jealous of others, you start losing the sanctity of your character. And character lost, everything lost. Be competitive, ruthlessly competitive but your competition should be with the person who you were a day before. I have always learned good qualities from others but competed only against myself. When you envy others, you don't wish well for them, imagine Alwin, how would you feel when your friends pray for your failure? The devil, jealousy, will stop you from appreciating the good in others and when you can't appreciate the good in others, you can't learn good qualities from them. You should resent and feel disgraceful if you are unable to be better than the person you were yesterday. If you compete with others, a point will come where your growth will get stagnated but if you compete with yourself, the sky is the limit and there will be no end to your progress. So, I would like to slightly modify the quote used by your teacher, it's not laziness but jealousy that leads to no progress. The more you start to appreciate others, the more will be harmony in your life, jealousy will only create stress. Let there be harmony in the world to save humanity.

(A huge round of applause came from the audience)

Alwin: Thanks a lot Anil sir, your message is loud and clear. Henceforth, I will be greedy but only to become a better version of myself daily.

Be competitive, be ruthlessly competitive but your competition should be with the person who you were a day before.

Key takeaways

Our biggest competition is with ourselves and not with others. Competing with others will result in stagnation while competing with yourself leads to lifelong learning. Greed for growth should be born not while comparing your life with others but while you compare your life with a person you were before. Comparing your life with others will give birth to a feeling of jealousy. When a person is jealous, he will waste his time wishing bad for others rather than trying to do anything to improve himself. A day without progress is a day wasted. The existence of progress is more important than the quantum of progress. Jealousy inflates your ego to such an extent that it doesn't allow you to learn good things from others and hampers your progress.

The best way to grow without stress is by seeing a teacher in every competitor. Just like how a child will never be jealous of his teacher for having more knowledge than him, similarly one should never be jealous of someone who is better. You can only learn from people who are better than you. Just like how a child will never compare himself with his teachers, similarly one should never compare his/her life with the competitor. Competitors are the best teachers, learn from them, implement their good qualities and compare yourself with the person you were before.

Celebrate every progress, no matter how small they are.

- Replacing a bad habit with a productive habit is great progress, celebrate it!
- Eliminating a distraction from your life is great progress, celebrate it!
- Waking up even 30 min earlier than normal is great progress celebrate it!
- Studying for even 30 min more is great progress, celebrate it!
- Exercising for even 10 min daily is great progress, celebrate it!
- Reading even 1 page of a good book is great progress, celebrate it!
- You don't feel jealous of others' progress anymore, greatest progress, super celebrate it!

Habits

Q. Hello Anil sir, my name is Roshni and I study in 7th grade. What are the habits that we students should inculcate in order to achieve success in life?

Anil: Hi Roshni, that's a very interesting question. Let me quote Dr. A.P.J Abdul Kalam who once said *"**You cannot change your future, but you can change your habits, and surely your habits will change your future.**"* To achieve success, one should have success habits. You get what you deserve and your habits determine what you deserve. Just like how taking a right instead of a left on the road can completely change your destination, similarly, by changing your habits, you can completely change your destiny. I attribute my success to the habits I cultivated when I was young. I picked up these habits from my senior at the age of 22 when I joined a company as a trainee and since then these habits have stayed with me till date. Friends, let me share some of the most effective habits, the so-called success habits that I have learned from my mentors. These habits have brought enormous prosperity and satisfaction to my seniors, me, and all of my other friends. I'm sure that these success habits will benefit each and every one of you.

1. **Networking-** I truly believe that all you need in life is one good idea, one good friend/partner, and one good opportunity to change your life forever for the better. That's the power of one. Just like how you need to pass your final exams only once to get promoted to a higher class, similarly, you just need one good person to get promoted higher in your life. Life is a journey and it becomes beautiful and easier when you are not traveling all alone. The more you network with right people, more will be your net worth. I have learned a lot from each and every person I encountered on the path of my life. I've had good experiences, bad experiences, and even worst experiences but every experience has made me better, wiser, and stronger. Your success to a great extent is determined by your ability to get along well with other people like your friends, teammates, supervisors, subordinates, or even strangers. And for this, you must have great interpersonal skills. People who are filled with ego, lack empathy and can never be good communicators. Jealousy and ego don't allow you to give importance to others. And, if you can't give importance to others, you can't communicate effectively. We all give importance to teachers because we learn a lot from them. Similarly, we all must give importance to every person we meet, and every friend we make. Roshni, meet more

and more people in your life, make as many friends as you can, you don't need 100s and 1000s of friends but only a few perhaps only 2 or 3 well-wishers are enough to add magic to your life. Roshni, finding good people in this world is like a treasure hunt, you've got to hunt for it. It takes time to discover gold. Networking is like hunting for gold and once the gold is discovered, happiness will be abundant. The more you meet people, the more will be your learnings that will increase your knowledge. Kind people will teach you kindness, smart people will teach you smartness, ambitious people will teach you to dream big, resilient people will teach you to never quit, lazy people will teach you laziness, losers will teach you to curse life whereas winners will teach you to cherish life, good human beings will teach you humanity, neglect the bad qualities and absorb the good ones, you never know which one quality might elevate your life. Meeting more and more people will give you access to wonderful ideas, you never know which one idea might elevate your life. Life changing ideas are all around us, infinite opportunities are all around us, all you need is just a small effort to shake hands with them.

2. **Lifelong learning-** I'm certainly older than all of you in terms of age, but I don't consider myself old because I am as updated as the younger generation. The best way to stop aging is learning. Lifelong learning will keep you young forever whereas anyone who stops learning is old whether at twenty or eighty. Successful CEOs and accomplished leaders of the world attribute their success to the fact that they never stop learning._Billionaire investor Warren Buffett once said that *"The best investment you can make, is an investment in yourself. The more you learn, the*

more you'll earn" Lifelong learning is learning beyond your formal education. Developing a new skill, learning a new sport, learning to use a new technology, reading a good book daily, researching a topic of your interest, learning a new language are all examples of lifelong learning. I learned social media so that I can connect with the outer world, I learned lawn tennis so that I can keep myself physically fit, I learned blogging so that I can use my words to bring some positive change in the world, I learned a new foreign language to boost my brain power, I read daily about all successful CEOs and entrepreneurs across the globe to get ideas that can help my company to grow, I practice guitar daily to improve my concentration, I spend ample time with my grandchildren to learn innocence. Not only in your personal but even in your professional life, lifelong learning will give you a competitive edge. Most of the employers these days are seeing lifelong learning as a core component in employee development. In most of the big organizations, employees are encouraged to pursue further education and it gets sponsored by the company. We do the same thing in our company.

One constant thing in life is change. Continuous learning will help you adapt to the changing world faster. The day you stop learning, you stop growing and if there is no growth, life becomes meaningless. All the students here, be a student of life because real life begins outside the school gate. Learning shouldn't stop after graduating from school or college because life offers more valuable lessons than school and college ever will. Step outside your comfort zone, explore the world, meet new people, learn new cultures, never stop educating yourself, learn new life skills, learn to adapt and most importantly learn to be a good human being.

'Live as if you were to die tomorrow. Learn as if you were to live forever'- Mahatma Gandhi

3. **Reading**

This habit is connected to the previous habit, in fact, it will help you all to pursue lifelong learning. I befriended this habit when I was in 7th grade, all thanks to my Dad who himself was a voracious reader. It all started with newspaper reading and gradually extended to books.

All the students here, how many of you read books daily? (*All students in the auditorium from 1st to 10th grade raised their hands in excitement*). Ohh, that's impressive, now let me slightly modify my question, how many of you read books other than your school books daily? *(More than 70% of the hands dropped)*

You all read school books because it is necessary for passing exams. Your life will begin to change positively when you cultivate good habits voluntarily and not because of forced circumstances.

Bill Gates, Warren Buffet, Mark Zuckerberg, Elon Musk, Oprah Winfrey, Shahrukh Khan, Barack Obama, and many other highly successful personalities in the world have one success habit in common, reading. Bill Gates read around 50 books in a year, Warren Buffet, the richest self-made investor in the world reads around 500 pages daily. Elon Musk, the most influential and inspirational leader of the 21st century taught himself to build rockets, surely reading has skyrocketed his career to infinity, I read at least one book in a week.

Reading is to your mind what exercise is to your body. Just like how exercising will keep your body fit and young similarly reading will keep your mind fit and young. If you think that creative thinking can help you prosper in your profession, then reading certainly can make you a creative thinker. If you believe that focus will help you fulfill all your dreams, then reading certainly can improve your focus. If you feel directionless in life, then reading certainly can give you a greater perspective in life. If you ever feel tired, reading certainly can destress you. If you ever feel lonely, books will befriend you.

All the strategies and ideas I implemented in my career to help my organization grow have come from books.

It is a little disheartening to see that the younger generation choose internet browsing over reading and social media apps over books. When I was young, there was no social media but today I'm quite active on social media but I haven't substituted books with Instagram. Reading habit is rooted within me and will remain rooted till my last breath. As a kid I once asked my dad, "how do I become successful in life" and dad replied," it is very easy, just do what successful people have done", "And how would I know what successful people do?" I asked, "it is very easy, just read about them," my dad said. And since that day, I developed this habit to read about people who made it big in their life.

I truly believe that society will progress if the people of that society are well-read. We encourage all the employees of our company to utilize at least 20% of their free time for reading. We even have a library within our company's premises to help our people cultivate the habit of reading. This library was built a couple of years back and ever since the employees installed the habit of reading within them, they have grown stupendously, both on personal as well as professional front. They have become more focused, productive, creative, patient, and most important, humble. The greatest quality that I've learned from books is humility. Reading helps you to stay humble, reading influences your thought process, it influences your behavior, it influences your attitude, and most important of all, it makes you realize your real worth. This world will become a better place to live, only when the people of this world change their thought process and reading can bring that change. Hence, I urge all of you to start reading at least 30 min daily. Read about people whom you admire, read about the skills that may help you to advance in your career, read books that will help you to manage time, read books that will help you inculcate discipline in your life.

Well, there are plenty of other good habits that all of you can develop to live a happy and meaningful life, but the next one, in my opinion, is the most important of all. Repay your debt, and give back to society.

4. **Give back to the society**

Winston Churchill once said, '*we make a living by what we get, but we make a life by what we give*'

If you are wearing stunning clothes, you owe it to the society. If you drive a luxurious car, you owe it to the society. If you live in a beautiful home, you owe it to the society. If you live a lavish lifestyle, you owe it to the society. If you are smiling today, you owe it to the society. If you are happy today, you owe it to the society. This society has given you abundance of joy, and prosperity, don't you all think, it's your responsibility to give it back. Your life indeed would be beautiful, but don't you all think, that it will become even more meaningful when you strive to bring beauty in the lives of others. Don't you all think that the charm of your smile will increase manifold when you bring a smile on others' faces? Don't you all think that the value of your life will become even more precious when you add value in others' life? Don't you all think that your existence on the planet earth as humans will get justified when you strive to bring a positive change in others' life? Because I think so, I believe so. There's nothing more rewarding than giving back and making a difference in the lives of people, or I would say in the lives of all living beings. Just like how a debtor in huge debt will be relieved of the burden and find peace after repaying the debt, similarly when you pay back to the society and try to make it a better place for all living beings, you find peace in life. There is nothing more satisfying than giving happiness to human mankind.

So how can we all pay back to the society? We just need the following three qualities that will enable us to pay back to the society:

- Integrity
- Compassion
- Helpfulness

The real essence of a successful life is a life that is lived with integrity. Unless, you are honest and a person of moral values, you can't give back to the society. Giving back to the society is all about doing good for others. Dishonest and corrupt people are too self-centered to do any good for others.

Until we extend our circle of compassion to all living beings, humanity will not find peace. We can never give back to society unless we feel the suffering of others. If you have compassion, you've got the feelings to feel others and these feelings will lead to the most important quality of being helpful. Help when you see people in need, help doesn't necessarily mean financial help but sometimes even a few encouraging words can brighten someone's day. Muhammad Ali once said, ***'Service to others is the rent you pay for your room here on earth'***

You don't have to be a multi-millionaire to pay back to the society, all you need is a compassionate heart. If you can't donate your money, at least try to donate a small portion of your time. Time is very valuable and hence we all want to utilize our time in the most effective manner to live a fruitful life. The best way you can utilize your time is by gifting it to people who need it. On Sundays, I love to spend maximum time in old age homes and orphanages. Earlier, often I used to extend monetary help until one day one of the caretakers there made me realize that the best charity I can do is by donating my time. Time invested for a noble cause yield much greater returns than funds invested in lucrative businesses. Start donating a very minute portion of your time for a good cause, a humanitarian cause. Volunteer your time at places like orphanages, old age homes, and animal shelters, participate in charity events if possible, feed the stray animals in your vicinity, be kind to your house help, and plant a tree. Time spent for a good cause prevents the growth of 5 devils.

You don't need wealth but a compassionate heart to pay back to the society. You don't have to do a lot but very little.

A little contribution of kindness from each of you can make a world of difference in the lives of many. You don't have to be an ocean but only a drop of it. Just be a drop in the ocean of humanity.

(The last line, '*Just be a drop in the ocean of humanity*' led to a huge burst of applause from the audience. Every word uttered by Mr. Suri was heartfelt, thought-provoking, and evoked strong emotions amongst everyone seated in the auditorium. Almost 90 minutes had passed since Mr. Suri boarded the stage and started his session but there was not even slightest of diminution in his energy and enthusiasm level. The audience seemed to be totally mesmerized and in complete awe of Mr. Suri's stage presence)

So Roshni, in my opinion, these are the 4 habits that all of you must cultivate so as to live a meaningful, beautiful and successful life.

Roshni: Thank you very much Anil sir for enlightening all of us with your words of wisdom. Surely, I will develop all these habits and will even ensure that my friends and people I know do the same. After all, to live a successful life, first, it is important to be a good human being. To earn success in life, it is important to pay back to the society. Thank you!

Luck

Many other students in the audience raised their hands and were eagerly waiting for an opportunity to interact with Mr. Suri. However, sensing the interest of the time, the principal steps onto the stage abruptly and speaks," Well sorry guys for interrupting such a wonderful session. I sincerely appreciate the active participation shown by all you students to interact with Mr. Suri and thank you Mr. Suri for answering all the questions so graciously. We all know how busy Mr. Suri is but, despite his hectic schedule, he managed time to grace this occasion. Sir, I remember telling you that even 60 minutes of your session will do wonders and you happily agreed for a 60-minute session, however, I just realized that more than 90 minutes have passed by, and looking at the enthusiasm amongst students, I see no end to their questions. It is totally up to you sir if you would like to continue the session and take more questions or shall we conclude the session.

To which, Mr. Suri very gently replies," I have always believed in under-promise and over-deliver. I'm enjoying my time here with these inquisitive kids. It's super fun answering their questions. It is said that a curious mind is never bored, looking at the curiosity of all these students, I'm not at all bored rather, my excitement level has hit the ceiling. Curiosity gives birth to ideas; good ideas give birth to revolution. When I came to know that in the past, famous sports and film personalities had attended the annual event as chief guests, I was a little apprehensive about whether the students would like me or not because I can't dance, sing or do any stand-up comedy to entertain, all I can do is share some of my experiences and my idea of 5 devils to prepare all the students for a better tomorrow. It is wonderful to see all these students showing so much of participation in the session. Let us not stop them and let this fun go on. Let them ask whatever they want. Through my answers, if I'm able to positively influence even one life here, I would very happily say, 'Mission accomplished'

But before we continue, I would like to take a small 2-minutes break to quench my thirst. As the level of questions are getting better, I need to recharge myself as I can foresee some interesting questions coming my way.

(A small break commences and the audience relaxes for a while)

After 10 min, the session resumes, and Mr. Suri gears up for the questions that await him.

Q. Hi Anil sir, I am Rahul and I study in 8th grade. First of all, I want to say a big thanks to you for sharing your knowledge and wisdom with us. I thoroughly enjoyed your 5 devils session and I could totally relate with it. I have an interesting question for you, I'm a sportsperson and the captain of our school's football team. I have played plenty of football matches representing my school, some matches we've won, some we've lost. When we lose, our coach says, "bad luck boys, better luck next time" Sometimes I wonder that despite working so hard, results don't go in your favor because of so-called bad luck, and sometimes, people don't work that hard but still get the desired results because of so-called good luck. Sir, what is your opinion about luck and what is the cure for bad luck?

Anil: Hello Rahul, that is indeed an interesting question. Nobody wants bad luck in life. No one wants to see the face of failure. Everyone desires victory. But be it a game of sport or life, sometimes despite putting best efforts, you have to deal with failures. In Bhagavad Gita, Lord Krishna said,"Karam kar, fal ki iccha mat rakh" You have the right to work but never to the fruit of the work. I know it might sound a little cliché but that's the reality of life. At least this is what I have experienced all my life that the only cure for bad luck is to work with all sincerity and integrity. The only cure for bad luck is to have this good belief that one day your luck will change. The only cure for bad luck is to never quit. There are innumerable examples in the world who turned around their bad luck into good luck simply by not quitting and working with more vigor. Thomas Edison took 10000 attempts to invent the light bulb. Giving up would've been the easiest option for him but his relentless efforts changed his luck. J.K Rowling, the richest author in the world known for the harry potter series, her first harry potter novel was rejected by 12 publishers, but her relentless efforts changed her luck. Nawazuddin Siddique is an excellent example of what rewards, perseverance can bring into your life. It took him 13 long years to get his due in Bollywood. Despite facing multiple rejections, he didn't give up on his dreams. His perseverance and belief that his luck will change one day indeed changed it for the better. History has proven time and again that perseverance never fails. The only certain thing about luck is that it does change my friend. Even I have seen plenty of failures in my life. Some of the start-ups that I invested in failed miserably. There was a time when I was almost on the verge of bankruptcy but I did not give up because I had this good belief that one day my luck will change. Soon one of my projects did wonders and changed my fortune completely. *Mujhe umeed se hazaar guna zyada mila.* It doesn't matter how many failures you suffer, all you need is one good victory to change everything. Rahul, to cure bad luck, we all need 4Ps in life: *Passion*, *Perspiration*, *Perseverance,* and *Patience.*

You don't succeed in life if you continue doing things that you are not passionate about. And you shouldn't worry if you fail doing things that you are passionate about. Your luck won't shine upon work if you don't love your work and you can never love your work if there is no passion for it. There are many people I know who do not love their jobs. They always complain about their work, their organizations, how unhappy they are working there, how unhappy and regretful they are not pursuing a career in their field of interest. And when their colleagues get promoted, they envy them and blame their so-called bad luck. Do what you love, what you are passionate about. If you follow your passion, you won't encounter bad luck.

The 2nd P is Perspiration. Perspiration can turn around your bad luck. As I said earlier, to cure bad luck, work hard with all sincerity and integrity. First, identify your passion and then start working. Nothing worthwhile in life comes easy my friend. You'll have to work, work really hard. Try working harder than what you did the previous day. Try outperforming yourself each day. Perspire every day and let your sweat shine your luck. But the best thing is that when you perspire for something that you love, you don't feel the pain, you don't find it burdensome.

The 3rd P is Perseverance. Your luck is bad, really bad when you give up. Your luck will shine when you keep trying. The bigger your dreams are, the bigger will be the hurdles. You've got two choices, either dream small or persevere high. There's nothing wrong with having simple dreams as long as they make you happy after all success is getting what you want. But if you have high aspirations, the competition would be equally high and to beat the competition, you need to persevere. There will be times when you will fail. There will be times when you will lose against others. But your game is not over, till the time you lose against yourself. Your game is not over unless you quit. All highly successful people from different walks of life have seen countless failures but their ability to not stop and keep moving changed their luck. Learn from your past failures and change your luck. Learn from others' failures and change your luck. Learn to never stop and change your luck. Learn to never quit and change your luck. If your dreams are simple, you might have to persevere less but if your dreams are big, the perseverance has to be bigger. Losers never start, thinking that they would fail, the weak succumb to failures mid-way and never finish. But winners never quit and overcome their failures.

And the last P required to turn around your bad luck is Patience. Great things take time my friend. Mahatma Gandhi said," To lose patience is to lose the battle" If you lose patience, you certainly lose the battle against your bad luck. The good thing about luck is that it does change but to see that change, one must have patience. Let me share an interesting fact about the Chinese bamboo tree with all of you. For a seed to grow into a tall bamboo tree, it needs to be nurtured with three things: water, sunshine, and fertile soil. In the first year of planting the bamboo seed, there are no visible signs of any growth. In the second year also, there are no signs of any growth. The story of no growth continues for the third and fourth year as well. But in the fifth year, a miracle happens, within 6 weeks of the fifth year, the seed grows at an incredible rate and becomes a staggering 90ft tall Chinese bamboo tree. But did the tree grow only in the fifth year and was dormant in the previous four years. No, the tree continued growing but under the ground. Though there were no visible signs of growth above the ground in the first four years, but there was an unseen powerful foundation that was developed beneath the ground. The roots of the tree kept growing and it happened because the seed was nurtured with sunlight and water all these years. The same thing applies to our life, keep working and have patience. As long as you are working, you are growing and your luck is changing to become better.

You may not instantly see the signs of growth or change but the fact is that you are on the right track.

So, Rahul, these are the 4Ps: *Passion, Perspiration, Perseverance, and Patience* that can change anyone's luck. In the end, I just want to say that work hard to impress the God above, work hard to convince the God above that, yes, you are worthy of success. To score good marks in exam, you need to impress the paper checker with the quality of your answers because it is the paper checker who has the authority to give you marks, similarly to turn around your bad luck, you need to impress the God above with your efforts. Let him be convinced with your work to change your luck.

(The audience loved it and responded with a thunderous round of applause. The audience got charged up listening to Anil's words that were filled with wisdom and inspiration.)

Rahul: Thanks a lot Anil sir. Your words are very inspiring and encouraging. Next time, if I ever lose a football match or score less marks, instead of blaming so-called bad luck, I'll rather exhibit 4Ps and try to change my luck. I'll work to impress the Almighty who has the power to change my luck at any time.

Key takeaways

"Work like hell. I mean you just have to put in 80 to 100 hour weeks every week. [This] improves the odds of success. If other people are putting in 40 hour workweeks and you're putting in 100 hour workweeks, then even if you're doing the same thing, you know that you will achieve in four months what it takes them a year to achieve."- Elon Musk

Fortune favors the brave. Luck favors the more persistent one. Sometimes failures are inevitable despite doing everything right but most of the time, people fail as they don't do everything that is required to succeed. Whether it is bad luck or lack of 100% efforts, the cure for both is to work more. We must focus more on what is within our control (like working) and less on what is beyond our control (like the outcome).

4Ps: Passion, Perspiration, Perseverance, and Patience are very essential for converting bad luck into good luck, sad times into happy times, and failures into triumphs. Unless you love your work, luck will never shine. It becomes easier to love your work when you choose to turn your passion into your profession. It becomes easier to change your luck when you put relentless efforts to reach your goal. You get closer to your destination inch by inch when you choose to overcome all the obstacles that may come your way. Having patience and not losing faith is extremely important to accomplish goals. Success is not achieved overnight, it has never been achieved overnight but has always been a result of accumulated little steps taken each day.

Lastly, work hard to impress the Almighty who's watching everything. Your bosses might overlook your efforts, your co-workers might overlook your efforts, your partners might overlook your efforts, your friends might overlook your efforts but the Almighty never fails to notice your efforts. He has the power to change your bad luck and will reward you with what you deserve at the right time. The only condition he expects you to fulfill is to just keep going.

4Ps

4Ps for Success

"How do I shine, how do I win",
a young boy asked his coach,
"I want to achieve greatness in life,
what should be my approach?"
Looking at your desire for Success,
let me share my expertise,
Time and again I have seen people prosper
having the following 4Ps!

Define your goals clearly and lock them in
your mind, With every step towards your
goal be honest, humble and kind.
Acquire all the resources required and put them into action,
Let me introduce the 1st P for Success,
it's called PASSION!

Avoid seeking shortcuts, give your sweat, tears and toil,
Don't you be at ease till you burn the midnight oil.
Be consistent in your efforts to leave a lasting impression,
The 2nd P required for Success is PERSPIRATION!

Countless hurdles and obstacles
will try to hamper your way,
After failing don't you quit, keep trying every day.
With tenacity and self-belief one can
overcome every hindrance,
Nothing can stop you boy, if you show PERSEVERANCE!

Rome wasn't built in a day, great things take time,
You will get wiser and better with every step you climb.
Approach for Success remains same across all nations,
Victory certainly will be yours my friend, just have
PATIENCE!!!

– CA Harshil Mehta

Five Angels

After giving a beautiful response to Rahul's question, Mr. Anil took a break of around 5-8 min. Almost 2 hrs had passed since Mr. Anil started sharing his wisdom and knowledge on the stage. Seeing all the other enthusiastic students waiting for their turn to interact with Mr. Suri, the Principal was happy looking at the active participation coming from the audience but at the same time was even slightly worried looking at the time. It was almost 11 pm however the event was supposed to end by 10 pm. 1 hr was kept for Mr. Suri's session but Mr. Suri under promised and over delivered. Even after 2 hrs, he didn't seem tired nor did the audience, rather Mr. Suri was excited and eager to take up more questions. Indeed, it was overwhelming to see his humility despite being so successful and busy in life. Success enters the head of many but only a few choose to embrace humility. Such people are worth admiring.

In the interest of the time, the principal steps onto the stage, grabs the mic, and announces," Hello everyone, I'm sure you guys are having a great time, especially the students. I like the confidence and enthusiasm with which you all are interacting with Mr. Suri. I appreciate the curiosity, after all a curious mind is a pathway towards revolution. Also, big thanks to Mr. Suri for being so patient and answering all the questions in a very beautiful and impactful manner. However, in the interest of the time, since it's already too late, let's have one last question, one last blockbuster question. Mr. Suri, you may select whoever you wish to." As usual multiple hands went up but Mr. Suri took his time to scan through the audience and finally selected a handsome grown-up boy wearing a black shirt from the second last row.

Q. Hello Mr. Suri, it was extremely delightful to hear about all the experiences of your life. Indeed, they are very enriching. I was waiting for my turn for quite a long time but I am glad that it came last. As they say, save the best for the last, I certainly feel that this question would give a perfect climax to this evening…oh I'm sorry, the answer to this question would give a perfect climax. I'm really impressed with your thoughts about the 5 devils that can kill humanity and to a very great extent, I agree with you on that. After listening about these 5 devils, a question has popped up in my head, like how every negative can be neutralized with a positive, bad force can be balanced out with a good force, good prevails over the evil, similarly, I'm sure that if there are devils then there must be angels. Who are those angels according to you that we all must have within us to fight these 5 devils and not let them overpower humanity? Whom do we replace these 5 devils with to continue to be good human beings, keep humanity alive and at the same time succeed in life?

(Mr. Anil after pausing for 25-30 seconds)

Anil: Hahaha…. certainly, the best has been saved for the last. Indeed, this is the most important question of the evening because you mentioned about becoming a good human being. Honestly, I never really thought about 5 angels as such. Always knew the devils to avoid but didn't really think of the angels to imbibe. Your question has got me thinking. Perhaps, has given me a new topic to give a presentation on, "5 angels", thanks! I might take some time because I'm thinking but I'm sure, I'll answer.

(After thinking for about 1 min…)

Words spoken in anger leave a permanent scar that can't be healed. Actions taken in the fit of rage often cause permanent damage not only to others but also to the person who acted. When I see people abusing others, being unreasonably rude, or sometimes even physically harming others, my heart cries in disbelief, for I would certainly break down if someone would ruthlessly offend me. After speaking to many people about this, I just realized that not everyone gets as affected as I do. And this is because not everyone is as considerate as I am. Not everyone thinks about others. Not everyone put themselves in others' shoes before attacking them. Anger along with a lack of consideration often destroys the relationship.

My Mom always emphasized on being considerate. Speak to people the way you want them to speak to you. Behave, the way you want them to behave with you, she said. Thinking only about yourself and lacking consideration is like adding fuel to the fire caused due to anger, the only way to tame the fire is by being a little considerate. The only way to manage anger is to pause for a while before acting/reacting in a fit of rage. Try to put yourself in another person's situation and ask yourself if you would be okay with such behavior. If the answer is not a complete yes for any of the silliest reasons, if such behavior could cause even the slightest offense, if it could even marginally upset you then it's time to pause even further and give it a second thought. This may not completely calm you down or rid you of anger but will surely dilute your harsh and inconsiderate reaction. It will surely prevent you from creating an irreparable damage. Uncontrolled anger can lead to arguments, physical fights, increased anxiety, depression, health problems, and what not, but only 1 minute of showing a little consideration can save you from all of this. So, uproot the anger seed and learn to sow the seed of consideration. After all *'As you sow, so shall you reap'*

I hope I am making some sense, do you all agree with me, especially the very experienced teaching faculty.

(The crowd responded with a big yes and the teachers gave a big thumbs up)

So, by being considerate and thinking a little about others before reacting can help mitigate the adverse effects caused due to anger.

Now, it's time to fight another devil which is even more dangerous than anger, **Arrogance**.

Nothing is permanent, not your money, not your body, not your looks, not your health, not your wealth. The only thing that can be permanent is your name and the respect you earn in your life provided you do something respect-worthy and people remember you for that after you've gone. In the end, people are not going to remember you for your money or your good looks but for how wonderful you were as a human being. And the quality of humility will make you all wonderful. ***Be humble to kill arrogance. Kill arrogance to be a wonderful human being. Be a nice human being to earn respect. Earn respect to live for eternity.***

I would like to ask all the students here, who would you all like more, 'the topper of the class who is full of arrogance or the topper of the class who is helpful, extremely kind and humble'?

(obviously, the response came for the second option)

So, friends, the best weapon to fight arrogance is humility. Accepting the fact that nothing is permanent and what you may have in abundance today will perish one day will make you humble. Knowing that not your wealth but your act of kindness shall be revered even after your death will make you humble.

Some of the most successful and influential personalities across the globe are admired for their humility, such as Mr. Azim Premji, Warren Buffett, Barack Obama, Dr. APJ Abdul Kalam, Mr. Narayan Murthy, Mark Zuckerberg, Ratan Tata, Mahatma Gandhi, and many more. The humbler you are, the greater heights you can reach for it is not the wealth but the respect from the people that uplifts you to greater heights.

Never let success get to your head because if it does, your downfall is certain. Arrogance will get you haters, humility will bring you respect. Your haters will rejoice in your bad times but only well-wishers will come to your rescue. Humility will make you a lifelong learner, the more you learn, the more you grow. Humility will teach you to be tolerant and respectful towards other, the more respectful you are, the more respect you earn.

So, friends, try to have zero haters, make more well-wishers, be humble and say no to arrogance because what is yours' today, will go away one day.

(Again, the audience loved the answer and gave a huge round of applause)

It was pride that changed angels into devils; it is humility that makes men as angels.
- Saint Augustine

Now, moving on to the brother of the 2nd devil, Ego. This is a tough nut to crack. It's hard to accept our mistakes because our ego makes us think that we are flawless. It's hard to accept that others are better than us because we think we are the best, that's Ego. It's hard to appreciate the views of our subordinates because we think we are superior to them, that's Ego. It's hard to climb the ladder of success because we tend to think that we already are at the top, but that's our Ego.

So now, how do we cure this disease of Ego that seems incurable? The best medicine to cure it is *'Awareness'*

The frog in a well thinks that he is the king. No one in this world is bigger, better, and wiser than him because for him his world is his well. He has never stepped outside the well and hence he cannot see the big picture. Egoistic people are just like a frog in a well. They refuse to see the big picture which makes them narrow-minded and ignorant thereby hampering their growth. People who choose to stay within their comfort zone are unaware of the world that exists outside their comfort zone. Be aware, that a bigger world exists outside your comfort zone. Be aware, that there are people around better than you. Be aware, that infinite learning opportunities exist around you. Be aware, that you are not perfect. Be aware, that you are not supreme. The biggest room in the world is room for improvement, be aware, that there is a big room for improvement within you. Be aware, that your ego can hamper your progress. Be aware, that your ego can ruin your life.

So step out of your comfort world to create awareness for yourself. Stop living in your cocoon. Stop living in denial. Be aware, accept, learn, respect, and kill ego to rise in life.

It's your ego that you are very strong;
It's your ego that your ideas can never be wrong;
There are millions like you in the big world out there;
It's your ego that you are the supreme and rare.

You befriend people who think alike;
say yes when you say yes and no when you dislike;
It's your ego to never bow and bend;
Life is precious, don't let ego put an end.

(As usual, the crowd enjoyed the answer, applauded, and became aware that they need to be aware of the fact that ego is dangerous)

Friends, now it's time *to* combat the deadliest devil of all 'Jealousy'. I'm sure that all of you must have heard of the crab theory. If you put one crab in a bucket, it will easily climb its way out but when you put more than one crab in a bucket, crabs will gang up and hold other crabs inside who are trying to climb out, trapping one another. This crab mentality is born out of jealousy. If I can't have it, neither should you; If I can't do it, neither should you; If I can't be successful, neither should you; If I can't achieve it, neither should you.

It is prevalent on social media as well. Whenever any celebrity posts a picture, I go through the comments section to see what people have written. Every time, I see a group of so-called trollers who troll that picture and waste their precious time making fun of that person. Some of them abuse, insult, criticize, and are very harsh and insensitive in their comments. I seriously pity all those people for the fact that they've become victims of this deadly devil, jealousy. All such ruthless comments signify nothing but jealousy. They are so busy trying to pull others down just like those crabs in the bucket, that they forget to uplift themselves. Pulling others down is not going to lift you up. As they say that the grass appears greener on the other side of the fence, most of the time we feel that others are living a much better life without knowing their reality and we start envying them. I believe this feeling of jealousy can be neutralized with a feeling of achievement. When you focus on others' achievements, most often you end up envying them but when you focus on your own achievements, you will always celebrate and rejoice.

Swap the feeling of jealousy with the feeling of your own achievement. The best cure for jealousy is to focus on your own achievements. Live that feeling, celebrate it, and immerse yourself so much into it that you are left with no time to envy others' success.

Ideally, instead of envying, we all should learn from others' success but unfortunately, rarely do I see that happening. We lose our focus because of jealousy. I strongly advise all of you to look out for the smallest reasons around you to feel like an achiever. When you feel like an achiever, you start celebrating it and the celebration invigorates you to continue the good work. You wake up early, that's a feeling of achievement, you score more marks than the previous exam, a feeling of achievement, you complete your homework on time, a feeling of achievement, you made a new friend, a feeling of achievement, winning a game of sport, a feeling of achievement, you read a good book, a feeling of achievement, you shed some extra weight, a feeling of achievement, you kept your promise, a feeling of achievement, you learn something new, a feeling of achievement, you do something good for the people, a feeling of achievement, etc. You see there can be plenty of reasons to celebrate and feel like an achiever. When you fill your life with an abundance of such achievement feelings, you stop thinking about others' achievements. When you start concentrating on your own achievements, rather than others, the jealousy devil is bound to die. Slowly but surely, you will get rid of this devil and would feel like an achiever.

So if you have this devil of jealousy, don't feed it by thinking about others. Be a little selfish, think about yourself, feel proud of the smallest achievements, and use your time judiciously to create more achievement moments. Do take inspiration from others but don't let that inspiration turn into jealousy. Just like how iron is eaten away by its own rust, similarly, an envious person is destroyed by his own envy. Hence, don't waste your time on jealousy.

Never underestimate the power of jealousy and the power of envy to destroy. Never underestimate that. – Oliver Stone

(It was 11:45 pm, but none of the audience members seemed sleepy. They all looked fresh, charged up, and deeply engrossed in listening to Mr. Suri. Now was the time for Mr. Suri to introduce the last tool to deal with Greed.)

Now let's deal with the last devil that is, Greed. Let's put the final nail in the coffin. Once again, I would quote Mahatma Gandhi's great words of wisdom," The world has enough for everyone's need, but not enough for everyone's greed."

Greed will eventually lead to jealousy and jealousy will eventually lead to greed. *Absence of gratitude gives birth to greed.* It's quite sad to see that most people that I encounter are always complaining about petty things. They always seem dissatisfied and upset with their lives. Rarely do I see people practicing gratitude. My Mom always taught me to be ambitious but at the same time be grateful for all the little good things I have in my life. We fail to recognize the good things we've been blessed with because often we compare our lives with others. We try to highlight what others have more than us giving birth to endless greed. The only weapon that can help you win the battle over greed is gratitude. As Zig Ziglar rightly said,***" Gratitude is the healthiest of all human emotions. The more you express gratitude***

for what you have, the more likely you will have even more to express gratitude for." You've got two choices, either keep complaining about things you don't have and make your life miserable or appreciate the good things you have in life, cherish them and always be happy.

Now whenever I talk about gratitude, some people think that gratitude can make a person ambitionless. Gratitude can put a full stop to one's progress whereas greed can keep the desire to grow burning. How many of you agree with this thought? (*This time a very few hands went up with a lot of hesitation)* Good to see some honest people raising their hands, and I'm sure that many of you would be of this opinion but let me tell this that practicing gratitude doesn't mean killing your ambition. Practicing gratitude doesn't mean you should stop working hard to achieve your dreams. Practicing gratitude is all about preventing yourself from altering your goals unnecessarily, practicing gratitude is all about saving your efforts from chasing wrong goals, practicing gratitude is all about preventing yourself from achieving your goals in a wrong way, practicing gratitude is all about preventing yourself from killing your own happiness and peace. Be ambitious but don't be greedy because where there's greed, there can't be happiness. With no happiness, there can't be peace and with no peace, there is no focus, and lack of focus needless to say what will happen to all your ambitions.

There are so many people in the world, who had everything and then lost everything because of their greed to want even more. Don't want to take names but I'm sure all of you would be aware of many such corrupt politicians, unethical businessmen, and scamsters who not only lost money, and power but also their reputation. In greed for money and power, people often end up spoiling their reputation. Never lose your reputation, it is invaluable. In greed, never lose your freedom and honesty, they are invaluable. In greed, never lose your happiness, it is invaluable. In greed, do not kill humanity otherwise everything will be lost.

So, friends, these are those 5 angels in my opinion, that all of us must have to fight the 5 devils.

Anger- Consideration
Arrogance- Humility
Ego- Awareness
Jealousy- Focus (on your own achievements)
Greed- Gratitude

MR. SURI'S FINAL WORDS

It's 12. Welcome all to a new day. From today onwards, let us all starve the devils within us and feed the angels. Before I end this session and head back to my home as my wife would still be waiting, I am a little scared like all husbands here… I told her I will be back by 10:30..nevertheless..let me share one small incident with you all, this won't take long, I promise. I hope you all are awake….

(crowd roared a big yessss).

A few months back, I visited the hospital to see one of my old friends. He is 75 yrs old and was diagnosed with cancer a few years ago. All these years he fought cancer and took treatment from the best doctors available out there. He is rich, filthy rich, so money is not a problem for him. He did pretty much everything that could help him survive longer. But alas…over the last few months, his health deteriorated very badly. No signs of recovery and hence doctors gave up and so did his family members. When I saw him, it seemed, technically he is lying on his death bed. His face was pale and gloomy. His body was very weak. He seemed very very scared.

I tried cheering him up, "Hey, don't worry, you gonna be alright very soon, don't lose hope, and do not quit because you are a fighter. I'm sure you gonna win this battle too like all the other professional battles you've won throughout your career" The expression on his face didn't change a bit so I asked," Hey... I can see fear on your face, what are you scared of, death?" to this, his expression changed a bit, widened his eyes, and got himself out of the drowsiness in a position to converse. He spoke in a very soft and tender tone," Hey Anil, no, I'm not scared of death, everyone has to die someday. I'm scared of my life after death" His reply perplexed me a bit. "Life after death, what do you mean?" I asked." Hey Anil, all my life I have made a lot of wealth either by fair or foul means, but today I realize that with all that wealth neither can I escape death nor the life after death. Lying on this deathbed, I've been thinking about all the things I did in the past. Though people around me might think of me as a successful person who earned a lot of money and lived a powerful life but the reality is different. All my life, Anil, I ran after money and power and in doing so, I left humanity behind. I've cheated many people and taken advantage of innocent people. I've been very selfish, greedy, insensitive, ruthless, and at times inhuman. Misused my power, and didn't help the helpless, though I could have, I should have. I'm unable to recall a single instance wherein I did something for others as a good human being keeping humanity alive. Jealousy, greed, ego, arrogance, all of this had killed humanity in me. All my life, I've been very rich but today on this bed I feel like the poorest person on this planet. Poorest, not because I have lost my health but because I couldn't do anything good and respect-worthy for humanity to carry along with me up there. Up there, in front of God, your good deeds make you rich, sadly I have none. The thought of how I am going to face God scares me. Why didn't I help people, why did I betray people, why did I break their trust, why did I speak to them rudely, why did I hurt their feelings, all these thoughts scare me to the core. On my deathbed, I'm going to die with this regret of not being a good human being. Despite, making a lot of money, I wasted my life."

While he was talking to me, he had tears in his eyes and that moment reminded me of Leo Tolstoy's quote.***" The sole meaning of life is to serve humanity"***

Friends, with, this I sign off now. I would like to thank Mr. David sir, for inviting me to this event, I thoroughly enjoyed each and every performance and I also enjoyed all the questions asked by these curious minds. Big thank you to all you wonderful, smart, magnificent students and your parents for listening to me so attentively for the last 3 hrs. I am overwhelmed with the kind of respect and love that I've got from all of you. I am not a famous celebrity or sportsman or film star yet whenever I attend such events, people shower me with a lot of respect and love. This makes me feel truly blessed. Certainly, I feel like the wealthiest person for I earn something that is priceless. Humanity is priceless and people who are serving humanity are the richest. Wishing all of you, an abundance of happiness and prosperity. Together, let's serve humanity, kill 5 devils and make this world a better place for you and for me, and the entire human race!!!!! God bless you all!!

The crowd was so ecstatic that they gave him a standing ovation with a thunderous round of applause. The applause didn't stop for almost 20-30 seconds. As they say, all good things must come to an end, the audience indeed was having a great time, but after the final remarks, some of the audience members especially the mature section became a little emotional knowing the fact that what the man on the stage spoke, does hold true but sadly very few in this big bad selfish world would value it and live by it.

Many a times, when we are watching a good movie in the cinema hall and having a great time, we don't want the movie to end because we are enjoying it so much. We don't want the enjoyment to end. But when the movie ends, for a moment we feel a little gloomy, knowing that the beautiful time has come to an end and it's time to get back to life, real life. The audience there had a similar feeling, an evening filled with laughter, joy, wisdom, and inspiration has come to an end. It's time to get back to life filled with hardships, struggles, surprises, hopes, despair, and the devils out there waiting to victimize you.

It was already past 12, but there was no sign of exhaustion or boredom on the face of Mr. Anil Suri. He happily met everyone, clicked photos, bid goodbye, and gracefully exited the venue leaving an important message for everyone; be a good human being; that's what matters.

People are often unreasonable,
illogical, and self-centered;
Forgive them anyway.

If you are kind, people may accuse you of selfish,
ulterior motives;
Be kind anyway.

If you are successful, you will win some false friends and
some true enemies;
Succeed anyway.

If you are honest and frank, people may cheat you;
Be honest and frank anyway.

What you spend years building, someone could destroy
overnight;
Build anyway.

If you find serenity and happiness, they may be jealous;
Be happy anyway.

The good you do today, people will often forget tomorrow;
Do good anyway.

Give the world the best you have, and it may never be
enough;
Give the world the best you've got anyway.

You see, in the final analysis, it is between you
and your God;
It was never between you and
them anyway.

- Mother Teresa

DO'S AND DON'TS

Some important Do's and Don'ts to make the most of your life: -

Do's

- Chase inner success, not outer.
- Have crystal clear goals in life.
- Discover your passion to have crystal clear goals.
- Understand your strengths, and focus on them.
- Put efforts in the right direction to get the right results.
- Be consistent in your efforts to get guaranteed right results.
- Your habits eventually shape your future. Cultivate the right habits.
- Value people who are helpful and your well-wishers.

- Associate with people who are smarter than you.
- Learn something new every day.
- Upgrade yourself with time.
- Spend your time and money wisely.
- Invest in assets. A genuine friend, which is so rare to find is a valuable asset.
- Do take care of your body, because your body is your temple. A healthy mind resides in a healthy body.

Don'ts

- Don't find flaws in your life by comparing it with others. You may not know the real picture on the other side. The grass always appears greener on the other side of the fence.
- Don't hesitate to try something new. The more you fail, the more you learn.
- Don't change your ambitions by looking at others, because it's a vicious endless circle. In the end, all you will get is a big disappointment.
- Don't waste time chasing or thinking about things that are beyond your control.
- Don't expect too much from others. Eventually, it will lead to disappointment.
- Don't put too much trust in people, be it your friends or relatives. Eventually, most of them will break it.
- Don't live life to prove a point to others, eventually, it will ruin your own happiness.
- Don't live in past. Bygones are bygones.
- Don't underestimate yourself, you can do wonders.

- Don't give up on hope. You are not a loser until you lose hope.
- Don't live life with regrets. The pain of regret is much more than the pain of failure. Life is one, make the most of it.

A Special day

In the previous section, we saw some do's and don'ts to make the most of our life. In this section let's see how to make the most of our day. Let me explain this through a small poem written by me.

The day you wake up hale and hearty, infused with fresh hopes,
Be grateful to God, for it is the day that becomes special!
The day you take baby steps that brings you an inch closer to your goals,
Feel accomplished, for it is the day that becomes special!
The day you value every second of your time using it productively,
Feel productive, for it is the day that becomes special!

The day you distance yourself from all distractions that act as hurdles,
Feel disciplined, for it is the day that becomes special!
The day you exercise despite all laziness trying to withhold you,

Feel fit, for it is the day that becomes special!
The day you learn some new skills in these times of obsolescence,
Feel relevant, for it is the day that becomes special!

The day you value every penny earned paving your way towards financial freedom,
Feel rich, for it is the day that becomes special!
The day you help selflessly giving happiness to all mankind,
Feel sacred, for it is the day that becomes special!
The day you do all of the above making your parents' eyes twinkle with joy,
Feel proud, for it is the day that becomes special!!

– CA Harshil Mehta

"*The journey of thousand miles begins with a single step*"- Lao Tzu

"Our life is the sum total of all the decisions we make every day, and those decisions are determined by our priorities"- Myles Munroe

- Start your day with gratitude. New day brings new opportunities and renewed hope.
- Inconsistency is an insurmountable obstacle on the path to success. No matter how tiny your steps are, do take them daily and march ahead.
- Value every second of your time. Go to bed with the satisfaction of "time well spent"
- The road that leads to distraction ultimately leads to a dead end. Distraction is short-term gain, long-term pain, the choice is yours.
- Exercise, exercise, exercise…at least for 10 min but daily exercise. Move your body, just move it!

- Be a student for life. Keep learning. Read to learn, observe to earn, seek guidance to learn, and apply to learn.
- Money saved is money earned. Bad times never announce their arrival *(eg, covid)* hence, respect every penny you earn.
- The entire day we act selfish, how about sparing a moment to be a little selfless. The entire day we do things for our own happiness. How about sparing a moment to give joy to others?
- Wanna give joy to others, why not start with your own parents. How about starting each day seeking your parents' blessings, let them know how much they mean to you, and give them all the respect they deserve.

THE SAND OF LIFE

Time is swift, will slip faster than you thought, Leaving you with deep regrets for missing out chances you wished you had caught, Time was never available in abundance to anyone, Wrong was your assumption for thinking that you had a lot!

Delayed actions won't help, for future is something you cannot see, Stop being haunted by bad times, for past is something you should not see. Forget past, forget future, Present is what you have at your disposal, Look around, it offers you plenty of opportunities with a lucrative proposal!

However, past wasn't a waste, for it made you stronger, Enlightened you with lifelong wisdom so you stay on right path for longer. For being happy, all the negativity within you must die, For being

successful, be resilient enough to give that one more try!

Today is the day filled with full of delight and hope, Daily investment of your efforts will yield great returns and has tremendous scope, So awaken the Giant within you to shine like a star outside, Enjoy every moment to the fullest as this is your life!!!

– CA Harshil Mehta

Chase a Rainbow

A Rainbow is indeed one of the most beautiful things that one can see in the sky and what really makes a rainbow so beautiful are its wonderful colors and rare sight. Similarly, I'm sure all of us aspire to live a successful, beautiful, and as colorful life as a rainbow.

Everyone does have a rainbow in their life to chase. Rainbow is like a set of goals and ambitions that we set and wish to accomplish to live a better, more complete, and successful life. But very few people actually manage to accomplish their goals and translate their dreams into reality. Because be it achievement of a goal or chasing a rainbow, both demands flying to the highest altitude, which is possible only when you keep fluttering your wings on a constant basis. As we know that it takes both rain as well as sunshine for a rainbow to occur, similarly it is our persistence, burning desire, and ability to overcome all the challenges that come our way, helps us to shine in life.

Since childhood, we have been memorizing the colors of the rainbow by its acronym 'VIBGYOR' which indicates its 7 colors which are Violet, Indigo, Blue, Green, Yellow, Orange, and Red. But when it comes to achieving a rainbow in real sense, the full form of 'VIBGYOR' is bound to change.

Here I am going to talk about the 7 most important qualities in my opinion that a person must have to achieve a rainbow in his/her life.

Victorious Mindset:-

Possession of anything begins in the mind. Though you might not have reached your rainbow yet but there is no cost associated with thinking positively and having a victorious mindset. Our mind is like a fertile garden in which whatever is planted whether flowers or weeds, will grow. So start uprooting those weeds that hold you back and start planting such flowers that will blossom into your Success!!!

Impossible is nothing:-

"Impossible is just a big word thrown around by small men who find it easier to live in the world they've been given than to explore the power they have to change it"—Muhammad Ali

During your quest for the rainbow, there will be certain circumstances and challenges that will tempt you to quit on your highest goals and dilute your focus. But do remember that Rome was not built in a day. Great things do take time and patience

combined with constant perseverance.

So if you ever find the accomplishment of a particular goal impossible, just look around, if you find people just like you who have achieved it, trust me if they can do it, so can you!!!

Believe in yourself:-

"Whatever a human mind can conceive and believe, he can achieve"—Napoleon Hill

You need to be a believer first to be an achiever. Never doubt your potential based on other people's opinions and criticisms. Doubt will keep creating a mountain but it's your faith that will tunnel through it.

Get up again:-

Failures are a part of life. If you don't fail, you don't learn and if you don't learn, you won't change. Failures are stepping stones to success. Nobody has ever traveled on the road to success without a puncture or two. Falling down is natural when you are on the path of achieving something new, something big, something extraordinary. Remember you cannot break a stone with the first blow of hammer. It may even take 8-9 blows, but that doesn't mean that your initial seven attempts were useless. If you have a 'Never say die attitude', you can rise to the highest altitude.

So friends you may fall down several times in your journey but refuse to give up rather get up again and you will still be standing!!!

Yet another chance:-

New day, new light, new beginning and new opportunities. Forget what happened yesterday because past is dead and no more in existence but present and future, both are alive and full of potential. You can still achieve what you always wanted to. A bad past was never a waste because it taught you many things that will act as a roadmap for your future.

Every new day is like a second chance that life gives you to fulfill your dreams so never ever lose hope. Forget the past, live the present, and build your future!!!

Opportunistic:-

"Opportunities are like sunrises. If you wait too long, you will miss them"—William Arthur Ward

There are plenty of opportunities all around us, it's just that we need to discern and grab them before anyone else does it. No opportunity is small as long as it helps you to make progress after all a journey of thousand miles begins with a single step. An opportunistic person is someone who will be far quicker than others in grabbing an opportunity at the right time.

So start exploring new opportunities around you, grab them, and make progress instead of making excuses!!!

Risk-taker:-

"The biggest risk is not taking any risk"
–Mark Zuckerberg

All the successful people have taken incredible risks in their life to make it large. Taking a risk is far better than not doing anything and regretting it later because not taking a chance at all will keep you stagnant for life. So throw off the bowlines, sail away from the safe harbor, swim against the tide, explore, discover and make it large!!!

Just Do It

Dreams are great, it gives purpose to your life,
They may come true if there is a will to fight,
Rise and march ahead if you want to shine,
No one ever prospered by wasting time.
Start taking small steps from now bit by bit,
Follow your heart, accelerate and Just do it!

Let no thought of failing deter you,
If your efforts are worthwhile, you will get your due.
You may stumble across some turbulence in your journey,
Don't stop, keep moving, keep up the energy.
Don't let a few failures dampen your spirit,
Follow your heart, accelerate and Just do it!

Life is like a river, you can't touch the same water twice,
Opportunities if not grabbed, will disappear within blink of your eyes.
No work is small if it teaches you something new,

Each day of learning will make you wise.
Dare to explore all opportunities and take its benefit,
Follow your heart, accelerate and Just do it!

Don't get complacent on coming a little far,
After all, you are born to shine like a star,
Sail off from safe harbors and swim against the tide,
The journey of success is indeed a roller-coaster ride.
Destiny is eager to embrace you provided you don't quit,
The best feeling in the world is, ***"Yes I did it"***

– ***CA Harshil Mehta***

No Risk No Gain

A person who risks nothing does nothing has nothing and eventually becomes nothing in his life. By not taking risk, one may avoid suffering and sorrow, but you simply cannot learn, feel, change, grow or love.

I would like to quote an anonymous philosopher who once said, ***"A ship in harbor is safe but that is not what ships are built for"*** Similarly life is not about staying in your cocoon or comfort zone and living with fear, guilt and inhibitions because that's not what your life is meant for.

Risk is a word that excites me and I am sure all those people who want to succeed in life will find this word exciting too because somewhere deep inside our hearts we know that without taking risks there can be no rewards, without taking risk you can't achieve greatness, in short No Risk No Gain.

Then what really stops us from taking risk. Why is it very few people have succeeded in life. If you see, the ladder of success is never crowded at the top. Despite knowing that risk-taking is essential for success, what really holds us back. Friends it is not about talent, hard work, or your potential but what really holds you back is your wrong attitude and mentality. Let me explain,

Risk has its own pros and cons. It can be rewarding or at times it can be disastrous.

People refrain from taking risk because most of them have a pessimistic outlook. They focus more on the negatives of risk and not on the benefits.

What can be the probable reasons for not taking risk,

- Fear of failures
- Fear of shame and embarrassment
- Fear of huge losses and criticism

But now let's talk about the benefits which I certainly feel are way superior and outweigh the negatives of risk.

Benefits of risk-

- It helps you to build confidence and develop new skills
- Unforeseen opportunities may arise
- It helps you in developing a sense of pride and accomplishment
- It fosters creativity
- It boosts self-esteem and makes you wiser
- It empowers you to break through self-imposed limits

After taking risk you may either succeed or fail but irrespective of success or failure, one thing is for sure, you will learn and grow, whereas by not taking risk you stagnate yourself.

So keep trying, keep making mistakes, keep learning, keep running as Bruce Lee once said, ***"Running water never grows stale"***

Let me give you an example of 3 eminent personalities who have taken crucial risks in their life and made it big.

Elon Musk: When you make millions on an internet company like PayPal, the world generally expects you to, well, create and make more millions on another internet company. But Elon Musk's dreams were different. Rather than following a more conventional career path, Musk took the money he had made at PayPal and invested it in two of his own highly innovative startups, SpaceX and Tesla. Though his attempt at operating these two ventures at once nearly sent both companies into bankruptcy, it seems to have ultimately paid off — today, both SpaceX and Tesla are thriving and Elon Musk is the wealthiest man on the planet.

Sylvester Stallone: With a baby on the way and too little money to pay the rent of his apartment, Sylvester Stallone sat down and wrote the screenplay for Rocky in less than four days. Producers loved it and offered him big bucks to bring the story to life, but Stallone refused to take any offer if he wasn't allowed to play the lead role in the movie. His stubborn attitude landed him a far smaller paycheck than what he could have earned for his screenplay writing, but the risk was well worth the reward: Rocky ultimately ended up earning millions of dollars and won the academy award, which skyrocketed Sylvester to fame. He went on to become an international icon, making hundreds of millions of dollars in his career.

Virat Kohli: On 19th December 2006, when Virat was playing Ranji trophy against Karnataka, a tragedy happened in his family, his father passed away due to cardiac arrest. His father was the sole breadwinner in his house. When you are chasing a profession of cricket which is full of uncertainties and the probability of success is so less, and to add more woes, if a family loses its sole earner leading to financial crisis, such circumstances surely demands you to give up on your dreams, continue studies and take up a job which is far more secure and safe. But Virat was too adamant to give up, took the big risk because he believed in himself, and as it is said *"Fortune favors the Brave"*, needless to say how handsomely he is rewarded for his brave decision.- millions of followers on Instagram, jaw-dropping net worth and of course Anushka Sharma.

These are just three but like them, there are thousands of other people in this world who believed in themselves, took some calculated risk, and have made it large!

Ever wondered, why Cricketers and Bollywood personalities enjoy so much stardom, get so much love from people, and earn so much respect and money, which commoners can only dream of, well it's because they all have taken incredible risks in life. Be it Cricket or Bollywood, both these Professions are full of uncertainties, and yet these people have made sacrifices, believed in themselves, and taken that leap of faith which others wouldn't do, and hence are referred to as "Celebrities"

The rule of life is, that for anything that has an element of risk, there will be a bigger reward waiting for you. The only question is, are you willing to take that risk??

Taking risk blindly or recklessly, obviously will lead to disaster, but taking small calculated risks in the direction of your goal will do no harm, it is going to be a win-win situation, you either win or learn and whatever you learn today will help you to win tomorrow. So what are you guys waiting for, throw off your bowlines, sail off from safe harbors, swim against the tide, explore, dream, discover, take some risks and change your life forever!!!

The Great Charlie Chaplin Speech

Many times, in life, you watch something impactful, learn something impactful, listen to something impactful and that impact is so profound that you feel like sharing it with more and more people. Whether it is an entertaining film or an exciting sports match or soothing music, you feel like sharing your experience with others so that others can too benefit from it. Before this book comes to an end, I would like to share a very powerful and thought-provoking speech of the great Charlie Chaplin from his film *'The Great Dictator'* that was released back in 1940. I feel that this speech resonates with the main theme of this book. Do not just read but try to feel each and every word and understand the emotions behind it. To experience the real essence of the speech, watch a video of the same on youtube. When I first saw the video, I fell in love with not only the speech but also the heartfelt manner in which the speech was delivered by the legendary Charlie Chaplin. Since then, I've watched the video multiple times.

The speech:

"I'm sorry, but I don't want to be an emperor. That's not my business. I don't want to rule or conquer anyone. I should like to help everyone - if possible - Jew, Gentile - black man - white. We all want to help one another. Human beings are like that. We want to live by each other's happiness - not by each other's misery. We don't want to hate and despise one another. In this world there is room for everyone. And the good earth is rich and can provide for everyone. The way of life can be free and beautiful, but we have lost the way.

Greed has poisoned men's souls, has barricaded the world with hate, has goose-stepped us into misery and bloodshed. We have developed speed, but we have shut ourselves in. Machinery that gives abundance has left us in want. Our knowledge has made us cynical. Our cleverness, hard and unkind. We think too much and feel too little. More than machinery we need humanity. More than cleverness we need kindness and gentleness. Without these qualities, life will be violent and all will be lost...

The aeroplane and the radio have brought us closer together. The very nature of these inventions

cries out for the goodness in men - cries out for universal brotherhood - for the unity of us all. Even now my voice is reaching millions throughout the world - millions of despairing men, women, and little children - victims of a system that makes men torture and imprison innocent people.

To those who can hear me, I say - do not despair. The misery that is now upon us is but the passing of greed - the bitterness of men who fear the way of human progress. The hate of men will pass, and dictators die, and the power they took from the people will return to the people. And so long as men die, liberty will never perish...

Soldiers! don't give yourselves to brutes - men who despise you - enslave you - who regiment your lives - tell you what to do - what to think and what to feel! Who drill you - diet you - treat you like cattle, use you as cannon fodder. Don't give yourselves to these unnatural men - machine men with machine minds and machine hearts! You are not machines! You are not cattle! You are men! You have the love of humanity in your hearts! You don't hate! Only the unloved hate - the unloved and the unnatural! Soldiers! Don't fight for slavery! Fight for liberty!

In the 17th Chapter of St Luke it is written: "the Kingdom of God is within man" - not one man nor a group of men, but in all men! In you! You, the people have the power - the power to create machines. The power to create happiness! You, the people, have the power to make this life free and beautiful, to make this life a wonderful adventure.

Then - in the name of democracy - let us use that power - let us all unite. Let us fight for a new world - a decent world that will give men a chance to work - that will give youth a future and old age a security. By the promise of these things, brutes have risen to power. But they lie! They do not fulfil that promise. They never will!

Dictators free themselves but they enslave the people! Now let us fight to fulfil that promise! Let us fight to free the world - to do away with national barriers - to do away with greed, with hate and intolerance. Let us fight for a world of reason, a world where science and progress will lead to all men's happiness. Soldiers! in the name of democracy, let us all unite!"

Credits: The Great Dictator (1940)- Charlie Chaplin

I would still recommend to watch the video because that is magical. No wonder, after listeinig to his speech, you all will find his words as relevant today as they must've been in 1940.

"More than machinery we need humanity. More than cleverness we need kindness and gentleness. Without these qualities, life will be violent and all will be lost"

Acknowledgment

The best moments of life are the ones when your dreams turn into reality. Today is one of the best moments of my life as my dream of becoming a published author has finally turned into a reality. A few years ago, I inculcated the habit of reading books as this habit is highly recommended by many world-famous leaders, celebrities, and successful entrepreneurs. After reading plenty of books, I realized that reading a book is a great source of knowledge whereas writing a book is a great way to express yourself and convey your message to the world outside. This book is my humble attempt to express myself and convey a message to the world outside. I'm grateful to the Almighty for giving me the ideas and strength to write this book. I'm indebted to my parents for their unwavering support and blessings. I hope that through this book I shall be able to make my parents feel proud. I thank my publisher 'Bluerose Publishers' for publishing this book. Also a big thank you to everyone whom I've met in life and learned something as I truly believe that life is the best teacher and everyone whom you meet in life can teach you something about life.

I sincerely hope that all my readers like the book and benefit from it. Fingers crossed!! Would be eagerly waiting for any feedback/suggestions that can help me improve my work. Hope to get more positive feedback. Again fingers crossed!!

You can connect with the author
at *'authorharshilm@yahoo.com'*

